THE
BLUNTED
SWORD

The Erosion of Military Power
in Modern World Politics

EVAN LUARD

I.B. TAURIS & C⁰ Lᵗᵈ
Publishers
London

Published by I.B.Tauris & Co. Ltd.
        3 Henrietta Street
        Covent Garden
        London WC2E 8PW
        England

British Library Cataloguing in Publication Data

Luard, Evan
   The blunted sword : the erosion of military
   power in modern world politics.
   1.
   2.
   I. Title

   ISBN 1-85043-

Typeset by Oxford Computer Typesetting
Printed in Great Britain by
Redwood Burn Limited, Trowbridge, Wiltshire

CONTENTS

LIST OF TABLES

Introduction: The Changing Nature of Power

In contemporary discussion of international affairs no word is employed so frequently, and so glibly, as "power". Yet few words are used so imprecisely. It is used by some to refer exclusively to military capability; while by others it is applied equally to economic or political leverage. It is used by some to refer only to power to coerce; whilst others use it equally to refer to the capacity to influence or persuade. Some employ the term to apply to an *instrument* of action, by states or individuals, a means that is valued only because it can procure highly valued ends; while others refer to it as the *objective* of such actions, valued as an end in itself. Few attempts are made, outside the specialised literature of international relations, to clarify these manifest ambiguities. And the word continues therefore to be employed, with cheerful imprecision, in a wide variety of meanings.

The concept of power, it will here be argued, is meaningless except in relation to the purposes of those who exercise it. The power to undertake an action which we have no desire to undertake, and would bring us little benefit, is a meaningless power. Thus the power of an individual to burn down public buildings or to make obscene telephone calls, though a real one, is valueless; the power of a state to ban all imports or to arrest all foreigners on its shores, though equally real, is equally insignificant. The essential meaning of the word is the capacity to secure, by one means or another, the compliance of others. But states and individuals alike only have an advantage in securing certain types of compliance, corresponding to their own purposes. When states were concerned to win territory abroad, it was reasonable to measure their power by their

1

capacity to do so. When states were concerned to win succession to a foreign throne, it was reasonable to measure their power by their success in that endeavour. And in both cases their capacity to secure their ends depended on their military capabilities.

The purposes of states in the contemporary international system are political. The leaders of states are no longer kings or aristocratic statesmen but party politicians. They are not concerned, like the leaders of earlier ages, to win succession to a foreign throne or to conquer territories abroad. They are concerned with the political character, the ideological commitment, of governments elsewhere. They seek to support the claim to authority of some governments (those that are politically congenial) and to undermine the authority of others (their ideological opponents) in the territories they control. This concern is especially acute in areas of strategic importance to them, such as the regions immediately adjoining their own borders.

The type of power that is significant today, therefore, is the capacity to influence political change in other states. That is a totally different type of power from that which has been of primary significance in earlier ages, when the purposes of states were different. The perceptions of the ruling elites, however, have not always changed correspondingly. Many believe that the means which were so often decisive in achieving the purposes important in earlier ages — means based on military power — will be equally decisive in achieving those that are important in the current age.

As a result the "power" of a state continues to be measured on the basis of military capabilities: on the number of nuclear warheads, missiles, tanks, aircraft and battle-cruisers which it possesses. The fact that most of these weapons are never used (and are increasingly unlikely to be used), since they cannot procure for their possessors the kinds of aims they pursue, does not affect that evaluation. Nor does the fact that where they are used (as in Vietnam and Afghanistan) they are unable to procure the results — that is, the *political* consequences — that are important to the states in question. Even the defensive capability which these weapons provide — their ostensible purpose — becomes irrelevant in a world where the attack against which they can provide a defence becomes increasingly unlikely to occur.

Such capabilities are thus irrelevant to the real "power" of a state because they cannot secure the consequences which are of importance to it. Those capabilities, it is true, could destroy all civilised life in the states against which they were directed. But this is not among the purposes which are held by any state (one reason why they are unlikely ever to be used). What they cannot do, as recent experience has proved, is to determine the outcome of the kinds of armed conflicts that do occur, or procure the purposes that are important to major powers.

Developed states no longer directly fight each other. They become involved in war today only in third states: almost exclusively in civil wars taking place entirely within the borders of a single such state (see Table 1). Those wars are undertaken in the first place by rival domestic factions. But the latter often receive substantial support of various kinds from external powers, especially the super-powers, sharing similar political ambitions. In such conflicts the fact that the intervening powers possess vast quantities of nuclear weapons, and every other kind of advanced sophisticated hardware, is of no significance. Most of that capacity is not even employed. And the intervening power may, therefore, in Afghanistan as in Vietnam, in Lebanon as in Nicaragua, find itself incapable of securing its objectives — the objectives that are of greatest importance to its foreign relations — by those means.

It is one of the purposes of the chapters that follow to analyse why this should be so: why military power should so often, in other words, be ineffective in determining the outcome of political conflicts. One reason is clearly that the means employed have not been appropriately adapted to the ends in mind. Habits of thought derived from an earlier age, accustoming ruling elites to believe that in the final resort a powerful state can always secure its objectives through the application of armed force, have dictated an inappropriate response to a challenge which is essentially political. At the same time the concepts and categories of one political conflict — the East–West struggle — are often superimposed on other conflicts which are of a totally different character. Because the image of the contemporary international scene which still prevails in the West is of a world-wide Manichean struggle between West and East, light and dark, good and evil, for domination — or at least a struggle to prevent domination by the other — political conflicts in other parts of the world are seen merely as component parts of that struggle.

So simple-minded judgements are made on the basis of the external, and extraneous, conflict, not the internal and substantive one. A Thieu, a Batista, a Somoza, or a Marcos may be supported on the basis of his position in the extraneous struggle (that is, as a good anti-Communist) without regard to the vulnerability of his position in the internal one (which may finally destroy his usefulness in the wider context). And because the confrontation between East and West is seen as a crusade, which must ultimately be fought out by force of arms, there is a temptation, when such figures are threatened, to believe that it is necessary to use military means to safeguard them (or to overturn leaders of other persuasions that support the other side). Yet the means of securing a military victory in such a situation, and above all the means of translating a military victory into a political one, are often not clearly analysed. As a result not only political but *military* misjudgements are made. For, as Clausewitz pointed out long ago, military power can be brought to bear effectively only if it is adjusted to clearly defined political objectives.

As a result of these over-simplified judgements, distorting and over-simplifying the true character of contemporary international society, errors of policy inevitably occur. Even from a purely Western point of view, such errors are damaging: leading, for example, to such debacles as the Bay of Pigs, Vietnam and the unsuccessful initiatives of the so-called Reagan doctrine. From the point of view of establishing a more viable international society, the misjudgements, and the actions to which they give rise, are even more damaging, since they inevitably accentuate the role of conflict and competition in international relations, and so reduce the possibility of establishing a more stable and well-integrated international society.

This book is therefore designed to consider the uses of

military power in the modern world. It examines, first, the way that power is exercised in the modern world and the dificulties of making it effective in many of the situations in which it is employed. It examines the way in which conceptions of power and power-relationships affect the attempt to secure understandings on arms control and disarmament. It looks at the increasing localisation of war, above all the fact that it occurs today mainly within single states, rather than between states, as was more often the case in the past. It examines the growing phenomenon of intervention by external powers in these local conflicts, which intensifies and internationalises them. It considers the importance of the preconceptions held by the superpowers of their strategic interests, which are now world-wide, in promoting such intervention, and the need, if the scale of intervention is to be reduced, for a more systematic effort to secure understanding between those powers about such conflicts. It looks at the role which could and should be performed by an increasingly powerful, self-confident and integrated Western Europe in the solution of such problems. Finally, it considers the deficiencies of the United Nations as it operates today in influencing the behaviour of states, and especially that of the super-powers, in their mutual relations, and the reforms in the structure and actions of that organisation that will be necessary if its role in maintaining the peace is to be strengthened.

Some of the chapters below make use of material that has appeared, in somewhat different form, elsewhere: in *Foreign Affairs, International Affairs* and a Fabian Society pamphlet. Most have been substantially revised for the purposes of the present book. The author is grateful to those responsible for permission to make use of them in this way. It is hoped that, taken as a whole, the book may contribute to the continuing debate about the role of power in international relations and the means of establishing a more peaceful international order.

1 The Erosion of Military Power

In the study of international relations military power has always been accorded a decisive role. Many writers on the subject have seen the pursuit of power as the primary concern of all states. An even larger number have regarded the "balance of power" as the crucial factor in determining international relationships. While there have been differences of emphasis about the role it occupies — seen most clearly in the sharp differences of view between the so-called "realist" writers and their opponents — the nexus of military power has been generally accepted as the most fundamental factor influencing relationships within international society.

The practitioners of international relations have generally acted on the same assumption. In their policies — for example, on levels of armament — state leaders have acted, consciously or unconsciously, in the belief that military power is the decisive factor in international affairs. To a large extent states have been classified on the basis of their military capabilities, with distinctions, for example, between "super-powers", "great powers" and lesser powers: a distinction related not to the size of their populations or the extent of their territories, but to their military capabilities.

There are a number of reasons for suggesting that this approach has become increasingly anachronistic. Changes, in recent years, in the way that international relations are conducted have made traditional ways of measuring power misleading. A large part of the military power that is customarily measured in this way has in practice become unusable. And the power that is really significant in contemporary international relations is of an entirely different kind, which is rarely even considered in such calculations.

A classification of states based on power capabilities was a reasonable way of viewing the international system in most earlier times, when the incidence of large-scale war was sufficiently frequent to make it a major determinant of international relationships. In those times the key relationships — the amount of territory states held, the colonies they controlled, above all their capacity to impose their will on other states — did depend to a considerable extent on their relative military power. Armed struggle was the principal (though never the only) way of resolving conflicts among states. When they did fight, moreover, they fought with all the military means at their disposal, so that their *maximum* capability was the decisive factor. It was thus reasonable to establish a kind of hierarchy among states, based on the maximum capabilities of each.

If these factors are of less importance today than they once were, it is not because of a sudden moral regeneration among the leaders of states, leading them to renounce war as an instrument of policy. At rare moments it has been hoped that such a transformation might take place. After 1918 it was held by some that, since the war to end wars had already been fought, it would henceforth be possible for international relations to be conducted on a more civilised basis. Military power would become of little significance, and states would be able substantially to dispense with armaments. The successive assaults of Japan, Italy and Germany during the thirties quickly dispelled that illusion. The use of military force by governments had clearly not been abandoned, and even peace-loving states found themselves obliged to arm themselves if a more peaceful and just international society was to be established. After the Second World War it was hoped once more, for a brief moment, that a more peaceful era would dawn, in which military power would count for less. But that hope too was soon to be dispelled by the new confrontation that emerged between East and West, and the re-establishment of an international system in which the balance of armaments was once more seen as of decisive importance.

The reason for believing that traditional assessments of power now require revision is quite different from this. It is not that the world's political leaders have been led to renounce war. Nor is it that a "balance of terror" has made war impossible: on the contrary, we shall shortly see that that balance has always been something of an illusion, and that today it counts less than ever in preventing large-scale conventional war. Military power is not about to be abolished, and it will certainly continue to have a major role to play for the foreseeable future. The balance of power in the traditional sense may none the less not have the primacy that has traditionally been accorded to it. Indeed, our whole conception of what constitutes power may have to be altered to take account of inter-state relations in the contemporary world. And new measurements of that elusive term may need to be established, depending far less than before on the overall capacity for destruction.

The decreasing role played by overall military power derives in part from changes in the *objectives* which states mainly pursue; and in part from the different *means* which they now adopt in order to pursue them.

The most important change concerns national motives. Traditionally states competed for assets that were in limited supply and could usually be acquired only through all-out armed struggle against another state. Competition took place, for example, for succession, the right to a throne elsewhere — probably the most frequent cause of war from the Middle Ages to the eighteenth century. Or, particularly in the sixteenth and the first half of the seventeenth century, states disputed about religion: usually, which religion could be practised in a particular territory. In other cases they fought essentially for territorial objectives: again, assets which both could not simultaneously control. Finally, in the nineteenth century many wars were fought about the right of people to secure national independence (if they were ruled by another state), national unity (if they were scattered among several states), or national preeminence.* All of these were *competitive* goals: they could be had only at the expense of another state. And they could

---

* For a detailed analysis of the motives of states in each of these ages, see Evan Luard, *War in International Society* (London, 1986).

normally be achieved only by war between one state and another.

In the contemporary world these traditional goals have largely disappeared. Among developed states today (and for the present we are mainly concerned with the policies of developed states) there are no serious territorial disputes; and even where they can be said to exist (for example, West Germany's desire for reunification, or Japan's for the return of the four islands lost to the Soviet Union), there is not the remotest likelihood of an attempt to resolve the issue by force of arms. The Soviet Union today, it is generally accepted, has no aspirations to extend her borders, any more than has the United States (objectives which could only be secured by the use of force). This is a major change from the situation only 50 years ago, when several European states were determined to alter the territorial *status quo* in their favour, by force if necessary. Other motives which formerly frequently led to war have today equally been modified or abandoned. The demand to promote or protect a religion, so often the cause of war in earlier times, is no longer powerful among developed states; and it would certainly not today be undertaken by war. Still less are states likely to go to war to determine royal succession in another land. The desire to secure national independence or national unity has remained powerful among colonial and ex-colonial peoples and has sometimes been the cause of war over recent years, but has not affected relations among developed countries. And even the competition for national status, though it still occurs, is not conceived in military terms or as a reason for war: status today is judged rather in terms of economic development, cultural achievement, sporting triumphs and other sources of national pride — achievements that are to be had without war.

In the contemporary world the essential subject of dispute, and of competition, among states is political. National leaders are themselves party politicians, deeply imbued by a particular political creed, and committed to a particular ideology. For that reason they care passionately about the type of political system that is established in other states. This is, admittedly, partly for strategic reasons: since they believe that a government of opposing ideology may be a threat to their own security. But it is very much for political reasons also: because they believe that one political system is *better* than another. A primary concern of most major states today, and the cause of almost all armed conflicts affecting such governments, concerns the type of government that holds power in other states.

Motives for war in the contemporary world

The importance of this motivation can be immediately seen from the type of wars that are fought.

External wars (wars between states) of the kind that were previously the norm, now hardly ever occur. Since 1945 no significant developed state has been directly engaged in war against another such state (China, which was engaged against the United States and other developed countries in the Korean War, was a significant military power but not a developed state). The military competition among major states, which had been carried on for centuries before, now appears to be largely at an end. In Europe there has been no war for 30 years, a longer period of peace than it has probably ever known; and in the 11 years before that only two occurred, both deriving from political conflicts and taking place entirely within the frontiers of a single state (the Greek civil war and the Soviet invasion of Hungary). Even among developing countries external wars of the traditional kind have been rare. Though the process of decolonisation brought about a number of limited territorial disputes, they were restricted in scale, being confined to particular frontiers or territories in dispute at the time of decolonisation (Kashmir, the Sahara, the Somali-populated areas of Kenya and Ethiopia, the China–India border, East Malaysia and East Timor, for example); or actions to complete decolonisation (Goa, West Irian, the Falklands). Almost the only external war of the traditional kind has been Iraq's attack on Iran in 1980. For the most part the wars of the third world, like the remaining wars of the first, have overwhelmingly been civil wars concerning the *internal* political situation in particular states (see Table 7 on p. 67).

Most wars in the modern world, therefore, begin at least as

domestic conflicts. This is scarcely surprising in an age of ideological conflict. All civil wars are "ideological" in the broadest sense; since they are all fought between groups of differing political aims and beliefs. Many of the present age are "ideological" in the sense most widely used today: that is, they occur between Communist and non-Communist, or at least left-wing and right-wing, factions. Of this sort were all the most important wars of the era: the Chinese civil war; the Greek civil war; the Korean War; the wars in Guatemala (1954), Cuba (1956–9), the Dominican Republic (1965), Nicaragua (1961–79 and 1980–), El Salvador (1980–), and other Latin American countries; the wars in Angola, Mozambique and other parts of Africa; the wars in Vietnam, Cambodia and Laos, and in Afghanistan in Asia, to give only some of the more obvious examples.

Such civil conflicts, like external wars, today take place in developing countries only. Though the leaders of developed states are passionately concerned about ideological or other political questions, they no longer go to war about them within their own countries or continents. In some cases such states are democratic, so that alternative means of changing governments exist. In others, as in Eastern Europe, the political system is so firmly entrenched, and military power so monopolised by the existing authorities, for there to be little practical possibility of effecting an armed rebellion. In both cases, the political systems are, for whatever reason, sufficiently stable to avoid civil war.

Wars in the modern world, therefore, *begin* overwhelmingly as civil wars within developing countries. But such conflicts do not always *remain* exclusively domestic. External powers, often the super-powers, frequently become involved, more or less deeply, in providing assistance to one political faction or another (for a list of super-power interventions, see Table 1). Each has believed that the control of the country concerned by the government of a different political faith could represent an unacceptable threat to its national interests, a challenge to security, a loss of face, or a defeat for its own ideological alliance, which it must do all in its power to prevent. Often such intervention is essentially defensive in aim. It has been

TABLE 1   INTERVENTION BY SUPER-POWERS, 1945–86

Date	Super-power	Area of intervention	Purpose of intervention
1956	Soviet Union	Hungary	To overturn Nagy government
1961–73	United States	Indo-China	To maintain non-Communist government in power in South Vietnam, Laos and Cambodia
1965	United States	Dominican Republic	To overturn Caamano government
1968	Soviet Union	Czechoslovakia	To overturn Dubček government
1979–	Soviet Union	Afghanistan	To overturn Amin and maintain pro-Communist government in power
1983	United States	Grenada	To overturn Revolutionary Military Council

Only interventions involving the use of the intervening power's own armed forces are included. In addition there are many cases of *support* for rebel factions involved in civil war, through the supply of arms and other assistance — as in Greece (1946–9), Guatemala (1954), Cuba (1961), Nicaragua (1981–) (see Chapter 4 below). US actions in Korea (1950–3) and Lebanon (1983–4) are not included, since they formed part of multilateral operations.

most strenuously undertaken to maintain the existing *status quo*, when it was believed that this was threatened by a change: as when the Soviet Union intervened to prevent Hungary, Czechoslovakia or Afghanistan from falling under the control of a regime which might threaten her interests; or when the United States intervened in Guatemala (1954), Cuba (1961), the Dominican Republic (1965) and Grenada (1983) to prevent the governments of those countries falling into, or remaining in, left-wing hands. In other cases the same purpose has been fulfilled without direct intervention by the external power, through the provision of substantial military assistance to rebels seeking to unseat governments of opposing ideology: as by the Soviet Union's allies in Greece in 1946–9 or by the United States today in Nicaragua, Angola, Afghanistan and Cambodia. In every case, therefore, it has been the domestic situation in another country that has been of concern to the major powers involved, not an external issue arising directly between them. Neither has at any time been engaged in direct conflict with the other. In every case their object has been to ensure that a government of a particular political persuasion held power in a particular state. There is every indication that this will remain the pattern of conflict for the foreseeable future. The major powers compete within the territories of *other* states: in a world-wide civil war fought mainly between local factions of their own political persuasion.

The essential change in such an international system is not that military power is no longer employed. A civil war is precisely an attempt to use military means to determine a political dispute; and external intervention in such wars is an attempt to provide further military means for determining such a conflict. The essential differences in a system of international civil war (undertaken entirely within particular states though with substantial involvement by outside powers) are two. The first is that external powers are in a position to use only a fraction of their total power in such conflicts, so that the *overall* power they can deploy is irrelevant. Thus in the Vietnam War — the most important single conflict in which the United States has been engaged since 1945 — the *total* size of US armed forces, the total number of tanks, aircraft and naval vessels at the disposal of the United States at that time, still more the number and size of the nuclear warheads and means of delivery that it possessed, was quite irrelevant to the outcome. In other words, even in that extreme case, seen as of fundamental importance to US interests, and engaging the maximum national effort, it was possible for the United States to bring to bear only a fraction of the power that it had so laboriously built up over the previous 20 years. The vast expenditures devoted to its armed forces during that time, the development of nuclear weapons, and of conventional forces of a complexity and sophistication never before seen, were of little significance in meeting the type of challenge which the United States then faced. Yet that is the type of challenge it is most likely to face in any foreseeable future confrontation. And it is therefore by no means certain that the type of armed power that the United States has been mainly concerned to build up — and by which its "power" is judged in conventional assessments — can afford it *effective* "power" in the type of conflicts it is most likely to be engaged in.

But the second, and more important reason, for the decline in the importance of military power in such a system is that the outcome of civil wars is in any case not mainly determined by military factors at all, whether of conventional or non-conventional types. If military power, as traditionally assessed, was the decisive factor, then the United States would have been quickly victorious in Vietnam, as the Soviet Union would have been long ago in Afghanistan. In practice the two principal super-powers of the world, with almost unlimited military technology at their disposal, have shown themselves unable to impose their will on relatively weak states in the most important conflicts in which either has been engaged over the past 40 years.

The fact is that such conflicts are determined primarily not by military but by *political* factors: the effectiveness and popularity of governments, the attractiveness of rival political creeds or political parties, the capacity to mobilize popular support, the standard of living of the population or important sections of it, the apparent dependence of either side on external forces, nationalist sentiment, and similar factors. It is for this reason that in many of the most decisive conflicts of the day — conflicts which have determined the entire political future of particular countries — the final outcome has been the opposite to that which the military balance alone might have indicated; and this has been so whether or not there has been any significant external intervention. So it was possible, for example, for the Chinese Communists to win the civil war in China against the larger and far better equipped Nationalist forces there; for the small and poorly armed forces of Castro to defeat the well-equipped Batista forces in Cuba; for the Sandinista forces to overcome Somoza in Nicaragua; or, even more spectacular, for the unarmed people of the Philippines to overthrow President Marcos, even while he still maintained nominal control of the country's armed forces. In all these cases the ultimate and decisive factor has been not military but political. All the extensive military supplies provided by the United States to the Nationalist government in China could not sway the outcome of the civil war there in the face of the unpopularity that government had acquired through years of corruption, inefficiency and rapidly devalued currencies. All the armed power in the hands of Batista could not keep him in power in Cuba when the people as a whole became disillusioned with his years of dictatorial authority. All the might of Somoza's National Guard could not maintain his position in Nicaragua, irrespective of the balance of military forces, once he had lost the support of the bulk of the population, including most of the middle classes. A large army, any amount of military supplies, the elimination of political opponents and the manipulation of elections cound not save Marcos from being swept from power when he found himself rejected by the overwhelming mass of the Philippine population. As a result the outcomes — outcomes of decisive importance for the future of their countries — were the opposite of what the balance of power in the conventional sense would have indicated.

In a word, it is the balance of *political*, not the balance of military, power which is today the decisive factor.

The power of the intangible

military power lacks INFLUENCE

These facts suggest that there exists in the modern world a vast gap between apparent power and real power; potential force and usable force. Much of the capability in which states take pride today is an unusable capability. It is not adapted to the kind of conflicts in which states in fact become engaged; it does not accord the capacity for *influence* which is the essence of genuine power.

All the significant conflicts of the modern world are not struggles to win territory, still less to win rights of succession, or colonial possessions, or trading opportunities, but to win political control, to maintain a *government*: as in Vietnam, Afghanistan, Angola, El Salvador, Nicaragua, Chad, Cambodia and many other places in recent times. In a world where the fundamental struggle is ideological, where the super-powers see themselves above all as champions of a particular political faith and the leaders of an ideological bloc, it is only to be expected that this is the form which armed conflict among states will now mainly take.

In fact, the political contest today is not only ideological in that limited sense: not only a struggle between East and West, Communism and democracy. New political movements have arisen — Islamic fundamentalism, radical anti-Western anti-colonialism, black consciousness and others — which are also engaged in conflict with rival political forces. These too sometimes undertake that struggle by military means. Virtually all wars of the age, therefore, including above all those in which the super-powers themselves become engaged, are political contests of one kind or another.

Power, therefore, today is the capacity to prevail in conflicts of that sort. It would be foolish to suggest that military power never has a role to play in determining the outcome of such conflicts. In El Salvador, Nicaragua, Afghanistan and Angola, to name only a few current cases, it is clearly the case that, over the short term, who rules may depend, at least in part, on the outcome of a military confrontation.

But, even to the extent that this is true, the type of military power which will be decisive in such conflicts is quite different from that by which the power of states is conventionally judged, and to which the military establishments of most states, including above all the super-powers, attach the greatest value. The outcomes of these contests will not depend on the number, and speed, and fire-power of their aircraft or tanks, warships or submarines, or on the degree of sophistication of the radionics and electronic equipment which they have developed at such vast cost; still less on the number and calibre of their nuclear weapons. Even among the weapons that are actually employed in such conflicts, it is not always the most sophisticated which prove decisive (as the experience of Vietnam and Afghanistan have shown). The military power which prevails is the power to wage effective guerrilla war, the power to make effective use of relatively simple weapons and equipment — above all the rifle and the machine-gun — and the capacity for movement and concealment within the country-side and within the major cities: to prevail in "low-intensity conflict", to employ the current jargon. In other words, it is the type of capability which the Viet Cong and the North Viet-namese, the Sandinistas and the Mujaheddin of Afghanistan, have above all demonstrated. This is not the type of capability for which modern armies — except, sometimes, one or two specialised units — are mainly armed and trained.

But, even if Western armies were trained explicitly for the kinds of conflict they are most likely to become engaged in — that is, for non-conventional, mainly guerrilla conflicts, in towns and countryside alike, rather than for set-piece armoured and air warfare — it would still not be sufficient to win them victory. The Viet Cong and their North Vietnamese allies defeated the US army and their local partners in Vietnam not because of superior training and tactics, still less because they were man-to-man superior. They won because they be-lieved in what they were fighting for in a way that US soldiers in Vietnam (like, in all probability, Soviet soldiers in Afghanis-tan) did not; and because they enjoyed (again like their coun-terparts in Afghanistan) the support of the mass of the people in the countryside, as the government forces and their allies did not. The phenomemon we are concerned with, therefore, is not simply a question of one type of military power proving superior to another. It is that what is decisive in such conflicts is not military power of any kind.

Military power of all kinds is relatively insignificant in rela-tion to non-military — that is, political — factors. Military success is itself dependent on the capacity to secure the support of local populations, on the willingness of these to provide food, shelter and support, to give or withhold information. Power stems ultimately from the thoughts, beliefs and loyalties of ordinary people. The capacity to win widespread political support, therefore, is vital not only to political but also to military success. Any worthwhile calculation of military capa-bility today — of the "balance of power" — must take account of these intangible factors, far more than of the total fire-power that can be brought to bear, or the availability of various kinds of hardware.

Such intangible factors are often hard to measure. A purely quantitative assessment of the relative power — in conventional terms — available to the Chinese Nationalists and the Chinese Communists in post-war China, Batista and Castro in Cuba in the 1950s, the United States and the North Vietnamese in South Vietnam, Somoza and the Sandinistas in Nicaragua in the 1970s, would in every case have calculated that the former must be victorious; and in every case it would have proved wrong. The outcomes in these four cases, leading to some of the most important political changes of the post-war world, occurred despite, not because of, the conventional military balance. The balance of *externally* provided forces is particularly often misleading. If domestic military forces can only marginally determine political change, external military forces are still less influential. However great their apparent military superiority, this will not enable them to prevail in face of the complexities and uncertainties of the local political scene. So Egypt was unable, even with an undoubted superiority of armed power, to impose its will on the Yemen in 1963–7, any more than could Israel, with an even greater superiority, in Lebanon in 1982–5. Even the most powerful states of all may today be unable to determine the outcome of such struggles. So, even after years of all-out national effort, the United States was unable to prevail in South Vietnam, any more than the Soviet Union could, after a similar period, in Afghanistan. The difficulty of imposing external military power effectively in civil-war situations was no doubt why the US Secretary of Defence is said to have opposed the despatch of US forces to Lebanon in 1983; why they were not able, when they were sent, to exercise any significant influence on the situation there; and why they had to be withdrawn a year later with little to show for their efforts. It is why the assistance provided by the United States, under the so-called Reagan doctrine, to rebels in Nicaragua, Angola, Afghanistan and Cambodia has proved so conspicuously unsuccessful (see pp. 92–103 below). And it is the reason why in Nicaragua today the direct use of US forces would almost certainly be strenuously opposed by the US Chiefs of Staff, who recognise that, though those forces could rapidly occupy the major cities, airfields and communication centres, they would not be able (any more than in Vietnam) to control the countryside where the mass of the population lives, except at a cost which would be quite unacceptable to the majority of the US people. Here is another situation, in other words, in which all the military might of a super-power is not able, even against a state incomparably weaker than itself, to impose itself effectively.

Finally, interventions of this kind may not only be ineffective in the country where they take place. They can be deeply unpopular with home populations, and so bring political costs of another kind. If a rapid victory can be secured, with few casualties, through the use of overwhelming force — as by the United States in Grenada and by the Soviet Union in Czechoslovakia — costs of this sort may be minimal, and there may even be some temporary popularity to won. But when, as is often the case, the involvement proves to be protracted and indecisive, the first euphoria rapidly wears off and enthusiasm turns to deep discontent. The spectacular victories — the Agincourts, Blenheims, Trafalgars and Alameins — which won glory and boosted morale during foreign wars in former days are not obtained in modern conflicts of this kind. Engagements are indecisive, arduous, frustrating and inglorious. The domestic political costs are particularly high in open and democratic societies where criticism of such operations can be made publicly and their horrific price is vividly displayed on television. A major factor bringing about US withdrawal from Vietnam was the intense unpopularity of the war among large sections of the US public; Israel's second invasion of Lebanon led to intense domestic controversy which helped to hasten her withdrawal. And one of the principal reasons why it is virtually impossible for the US President today (irrespective of his personal views) to commit US forces to fight in Nicaragua is that he is aware from successive opinion polls (as rulers in former days could never be) that the majority of US public opinion has consistently opposed such a step. But even less democratic regimes are affected by the same factor. Egypt's adventure in Yemen, Libya's in Chad, and the Soviet Union's in Afghanistan, among others, all became the subject of widespread popular discontent at home: discontent which was serious enough to become a major concern to their governments and to bring about some rethinking of policy and, in the first two cases at least, eventual withdrawal. The unpopularity of such actions at home is thus another factor which reduces the scope for the use of force in the modern international system.

But, even if widespread domestic support for such an operation is maintained, even if military assistance of the right kind — adapted, that is, to the waging of guerrilla warfare — is provided, even if it is provided to rebel forces that have some genuine credibility among the people concerned, and even if it finally proves successful, military victory itself is not enough. Military victory is only a *means* towards political victory, and it is not itself sufficient to win such a victory. The combined forces of France, Britain and Israel were not able, for all their military success, to impose their will on Egypt in 1956. Nor could well-armed French forces impose continued French rule on Indo-China and Algeria by military means against the will of the mass of the population of those countries. The troops of Smith and Muzorewa were generally victorious over those of Mugabe and Nkomo, but they could not keep political power for their leaders. The troops of Israel could win set-piece confrontations against any other force they confronted in Lebanon; but could not win any degree of political influence there (any more than could the US marines). The troops of Botha can always dispose of marching demonstrators or captured terrorists; but they are unlikely to be able to maintain the political *status quo* in South Africa. In many cases, therefore, even where military power *is* apparently successful, it does not succeed in determining the long-term political outcome — the outcome which finally matters.

Conclusion: power and politics

The conclusion must be, therefore, that in many cases where military power is used in conflicts within states it is often not the ultimate determinant of events.

In conflicts *between* states, it is today still less influential. This is most self-evidently true among those states, the great majority, which are for the most part on reasonably friendly

terms, and between which the possibility of war is barely
conceivable. When states have for many years enjoyed peaceful relations with each other — and that is true of most states in
the world today — a superiority of military power will not
affect the outcome of disagreements. Whether the EEC countries impose protection on US agricultural products, whether
West Germany agrees to the construction of a Soviet gas
pipeline, whether France accepts the integrated framework of
NATO, whether Turkey withdraws from Cyprus, or Greece
co-operates with NATO over Aegean air space will not be in
any way influenced by power factors. Even where the disparity
in military power is very great, it will bring little or no influence
in most cases: whether Mexico repays its debts, whether Pakistan becomes a nuclear power, whether Israel withdraws from
the West Bank or Syria from Lebanon, is not dependent on the
balance of military power between these states and the United
States. In these and many other cases, the military power of the
United States is of no value to it because it is in practice
unusable power. In these cases too, as in the cases of domestic
conflict considered earlier, it is political power — that is,
influence — not armed power which is decisive. This represents a crucial difference from, for example, the nineteenth
century. In that age, though war was relatively rare (Britain
fought only one war in Europe between 1815 and 1914), it
remained always a real possibility; and the consciousness of
that possibility influenced the actions of states. Though power
for the most part was held only in reserve, it was used sufficiently often, even against "friendly" countries, to maintain
its credibility. Today, among most states it is not used at all;
and therefore ceases to be a credible, and so a significant,
influence on relationships.

Even among antagonists it has on most questions little influence. For here too there is no real belief that it will be mobilised. Whether the Soviet Union withdraws from Eastern
Europe or Afghanistan, whether it improves its human-rights
record or allows more Jews to emigrate, whether it increases
the level of its armaments, even whether it intervenes in civil
conflicts in Africa or Asia, is unlikely to be significantly
affected by the overall balance of power between East and

West. On all these questions it is the political rather than the military constraints, the political rather than the military opportunities, which will be decisive. Even if the West were overwhelmingly more powerful than the Soviet Union, the attractions to the latter of giving assistance to rebels in El Salvador, or helping governments in Afghanistan and Cambodia, would not be significantly altered. And it is these kinds of action which, whatever the overall balance of power between East and West, are likely to be most favoured by the Soviet Union, since they provide the greatest opportunity to influence the political situiation in another country at the minimum military risk or cost.

The Soviet Union is equally unable to influence the developments that matter to it — for example, political developments in Western Europe, or US actions in other parts of the world — by the level of its own military power. In Europe even if local Soviet military dominance were to come about — and there is no likelihood that the West will permit it — it would not easily be translated into political dominance. The need to maintain a balance in the level of forces between East and West — a balance which (as we shall see in the next chapter) needs to be maintained at every level — will of course remain. But it is a balance required for military not political reasons: to guard against the unlikely danger of war itself. The military balance does not determine the political relationship between the two sides. On the contrary, it is the military relationship that is conditioned by political factors. In the final resort, the Soviet Union's military capability is limited by the credibility which its political system enjoys, above all in Western Europe. For this reason fears that Western Europe might, if the balance of military power were allowed to alter, slip irreversibly under Soviet influence ("Finlandisation") are exaggerated (and may even exaggerate the degree to which Finland itself has been subjected to Soviet influence by fear of superior Soviet military power). The reason why the threat of a Soviet military assault on Western Europe — occasionally held out as an awful warning by cold warriors in the West — is not a very real one, lies primarily in the knowledge, in the East even more than in the West, that a purely military victory, even assuming that it could be secured, would not be sufficient to win a political victory as well. And it is the political victory that — to both sides — is ultimately decisive.

Still less can the level of Soviet power influence US action in other parts of the world. It cannot in any way affect the degree of support which the United States gives, for example, to government forces in El Salvador or rebel forces in Nicaragua, to government forces in the Philippines or rebel forces in Angola, or the success which those actions achieve. The Soviet Union's possession of nuclear weapons, of a vast array of missiles and aircraft, or innumerable tanks and powerful warships, will be altogether without effect on the outcome of those conflicts. They are relevant only to a type of military engagement which is virtually inconceivable today, which bears no relationship to the reality of modern world politics and which corresponds to no imaginable national interest of either side: an all-out attack by the Soviet Union against Western Europe or by the United States against the East. The conflicts which in fact occur take place only *within* states, mainly in the third world. It is these which are, rightly, seen as important, since they can determine the political future of particular countries and so the balance of power throughout the world. But success in such conflicts is determined by a totally different type of power from that which major states have devoted themselves to acquiring and by which their strength is customarily measured.

In other words, power in modern international relations is no longer primarily a military factor. Increasingly we live in a world of political, not military, conflicts. And it is *political* power — political skills and political influence — not brute military power which is ultimately decisive in these contests.

2 The Irrelevance of Nuclear Weapons

It is in relation to nuclear weapons that the declining value of military power in the modern world is most obvious.

Over the past 40 years military power has been measured above all in terms of nuclear capability. The power of major states has been judged primarily on the basis of the number and calibre of the nuclear warheads they possess; and the range, reliability, accuracy and invulnerability of their means of delivery. Vast sums are spent by the principal nuclear powers in continually extending, modernising and otherwise improving these weapons; partly, but not exclusively, in order to match improvements which, it is believed, have been achieved by the other side. Sums almost as vast are spent by lesser nuclear powers in the attempt to remain credible nuclear states. And non-nuclear powers spend equally astronomical amounts — proportionately speaking — in order to raise themselves to the status of the former.

But how far do these weapons in fact provide their owners with any genuine measure of power? As we have seen, power in international relations means above all the capacity to secure compliance by other states: that is, to exercise decisive influence on their actions. And military power means capacity to exercise military influence: that is, coercive influence on those actions. But there is genuine reason to doubt whether the size of nuclear armouries gives any indication of the capacity of one state to influence another. Power, to be effective, must be credible. If there exists no belief that nuclear weapons will or can be used, they do not confer the capacity to influence, and so are not a component of effective power.

Some evidence of this is provided by those cases where nuclear states have been engaged in conflict with non-nuclear states. The outcome of the Vietnam War was seen by many in the United States, including its administration, as vital to US interests. Defeat, it was believed, would not only bring a substantial access of Communist strength throughout Vietnam and the rest of Indo-China; it could have repercussions throughout South-East Asia and beyond. It would represent the spectacle of a successful external aggression being allowed to succeed; of a friendly, pro-Western government being over-whelmed by an anti-Western Communist state; of an extension of Soviet and/or Chinese power in a strategically important part of the world; and of a major defeat, political as well as military, for the United States itself. Vital national interests were therefore believed to be at stake. Yet, for all the import-ance that was attached to it, there was never any serious thought that the United States might make use of the nuclear superiority it possessed against North Vietnam. More signifi-cantly, it would appear that there was no serious fear in North Vietnam that the United States would employ that power. The result was that a non-nuclear power was enabled to attain a victory over a nuclear power. The power which nuclear weapons are said to afford to those who possess them, in other words, was proved in that case ineffective.

Of course, it is said that nuclear weapons are not intended for use in a conflict of that kind; nor indeed for use at all. They are intended, it is widely maintained, to deter; and it is their *possession* rather than their use which accords power, since that alone may deter the use of force by other states. Yet in the Vietnam War they did not even succeed in deterring. In theory it is precisely in a contest between a nuclear and a non-nuclear power that their deterrent power should be most credible, since in that case the power possessing nuclear weapons need not fear retaliation in kind. Yet in Vietnam they exercised no such power. In other words they gave no influence to the country which possessed them in the type of conflict most characteristic of the modern world. Nor was this an isolated or exceptional case. The Chinese were not deterred from in-tervening with massive conventional forces in the Korean War by the knowledge that the United States possessed nuclear weapons. The FLN in Algeria was not deterred from attacking French forces there by France's possession of atomic weapons; so that, there too, a nuclear power suffered an apparent defeat by a non-nuclear force. Argentina was not deterred by Britain's nuclear capability from invading the Falkland Islands in 1982. In other words, even in those cases where it should have been most effective, because most credible — in a conflict waged against a nuclear power by a non-nuclear power — deterrence failed.

Most will accept that the decision of the nuclear powers not to make use of nuclear weapons in those cases (even though in two of them they incurred defeat as a result) was correct. The costs involved in their use, in lives lost and reputation forgone, would have far outweighed any gains likely to be won by using them. Even a *threat* to use them would have had heavy political costs; and would have weakened rather than strengthened the power employing it when the bluff was finally exposed. The non-nuclear power concerned therefore proved entirely justified in its assumption that it had no need to fear nuclear retaliation in these conflicts.

But these represent the typical military conflicts of the age. Thus, for the foreseeable future, in any other war in which a nuclear power becomes engaged against a non-nuclear power similar considerations will hold good. It will never be believed that, given the political costs of making use of nuclear weapons, given the universal odium that would attach to any power launching a first-strike nuclear attack, above all against a non-nuclear state, and given the precedent set for future conflicts of all kinds, their use could be justified. There is thus no likelihood that a possessor of nuclear weapons engaged in conflicts with a non-nuclear state will make use of those weapons, even in the face of near-defeat. In the kinds of conflict which mainly occur in the modern world, therefore, nuclear weapons are universally seen (like bacteriological or nerve-gas weapons) as *too* powerful to be employed. Thus their possession will not affect the result of such wars. And the balance of nuclear power is shown as irrelevant to the outcome of those conflicts which mainly occur today.

But nuclear weapons, it will be argued, were never expected to affect the outcome of "minor" conflicts of this kind (though, since all real-life wars, in the modern world, are "minor" conflicts of that sort, this could be said to reduce seriously their significance). They are relevant, it will be said, only to the outcome of the most important confrontation of all: that between the principal nuclear powers themselves. And their importance is not in enabling such wars to be fought more efficiently (and so giving greater "power" to those which have the biggest and best such weapons) but in preventing any such wars being fought at all. Once again, their significance lies in their *deterrent* power.

But in fact their deterrent power in such conflicts is even less than in those involving non-nuclear states. For such deterrence requires a belief that the country seeking to exercise it is willing to risk the destruction of its major cities and a substantial part of its population for the sake of resisting a major onslaught, even if undertaken with conventional weapons alone. So long as only one super-power possessed nuclear weapons, or so long as one maintained an overwhelming superiority in the power to deliver them, there continued to be some credibility in such a threat. It was not altogether inconceivable that, rather than undergo humiliating defeat in all-out conventional war, it might be willing to deploy nuclear weapons, perhaps on a restricted scale or for demonstrative purposes only, confident in the knowledge that they could not be used against itself: atomic weapons (even if of far lesser calibre) had after all been used against a state unable to reply in kind in 1945. *One-sided* deterrence therefore retained some kind of credibility.

But as soon as anything like parity in nuclear capability came about, as soon as each side was in a position to wreak unacceptable damage and casualties upon the other, if necessary in a retaliatory second strike, the deterrent power of such weapons was largely destroyed. A threat that a country will, if attacked, commit suicide is not one that will normally be believed. It was increasingly incredible that, if faced with a major conventional onslaught, even if confronting the possibility of defeat, any state or group of states would deliberately decide on a policy which must lead to an even *vaster* disaster, infinitely greater death and destruction, than that which defeat alone would entail. For deterrence was now no longer one-sided but two-sided. Retaliation with nuclear weapons against a purely conventional attack was itself deterred by the nuclear weapons available to the other side; and that response was deterred far more efficiently than the conventional attack itself could be deterred by an unbelievable threat to cross the nuclear threshold. Deterrence was negated by double deterrence.

On these grounds, the threat by NATO states that they will respond if necessary to a purely conventional attack with a nuclear retaliation is (whether or not it is immoral, as many believe) clearly irrational and counter-productive. It is a threat that has no military significance because it is totally unbelievable. No Soviet leader, if contemplating an attack against a Western target, would be deterred by such a transparent hoax. To base the defence of the West on a poker-player's bluff is a dangerous folly. This is so not only because in the final resort the bluff may be called, but, even more, because it is a bluff by which we shall not deceive our enemies but may deceive ourselves: into believing that we are more secure than we are, that a limited investment in nuclear weapons is all that is necessary to buy security.

That threat is especially unbelievable in the particular circumstances of the current East–West relationship. For the West's main strategic power remains today in the hands of the United States. But the territories that power would be defending from attack lie in Europe. Whatever likelihood there might be that a state would bring about the destruction of most if its cities and of much of its population to defend its own territory (a likelihood which itself is slight), it is even less credible that it would do so for the sake of defending the territory of *other* states three or four thousand miles away: that the United States would risk a strike by Soviet strategic nuclear weapons against highly vulnerable US cities for the sake of resisting a purely conventional attack on, say, Greek or Norwegian or Turkish territory. Because European nuclear weapons are not (at present at least) sufficient to represent a credible counter to the nuclear forces available to the Soviet Union, a purely conventional attack is even less likely in Europe than elsewhere, therefore, to be deterred by the balance of nuclear power.

The doctrine of "flexible response", though intended to restore credibility to deterrence, has not altered this fundamental dilemma. In theory, the existence of a range of nuclear options (from small-scale "tactical" weapons, including nuclear bombs, mines and artillery shells, to short-range intermediate missiles with a range of 500–1000 km; intermediate missiles with a range of 1000–5500 km; "forward-based systems" such as nuclear-capable F111 bombers; air- and sea-launched Cruise missiles; the French and British nuclear forces; Polaris, Poseidon and Trident submarines; and, ultimately, intercontinental strategic missiles) makes the threat of nuclear retaliation more credible. It is argued that, even if there were reasonable doubts about the willingness of the West to launch the full panoply of nuclear armaments in response to a purely conventional attack, a threat to retaliate to such an attack with nuclear weapons at the lower end of the spectrum could not be easily dismissed (whether or not any such intention really existed). But the fact is that all are aware that the only credible break in the entire continuum from low-level conventional war (and any war in Europe is likely to begin, and quite probably remain, a limited low-level operation confined to a specific target) to a full-scale strategic exchange lies at the point between high-intensity conventional and low-intensity nuclear warfare. Few would believe that, once the barrier was broken, any credible restraint could be maintained; and accordingly a willingness to initiate the use of nuclear weapons of any kind will continue to be doubted. Such doubts would be especially great when it was recalled that any decision to use such weapons in Europe would require the consent of a number of governments: the governments whose populations would be most directly at risk if the fateful decision to cross the nuclear threshold were taken.* On these grounds it seems

---

* According to the Athens guidelines adopted by NATO in 1962, there would be consultations among NATO governments only "time and circumstances permitting". This is, however, the publicly advertised position, adopted precisely to overcome doubts about the credibility of a

doubtful whether the doctrine of flexible response makes the threat to use nuclear weapons against a purely conventional attack any more credible than before.

If the peace of Europe is dependent, therefore, on some form of deterrence, it seems most unlikely that nuclear weapons are able to afford it.

Defence in place of deterrence

The effect of nuclear stalemate is therefore not deterrence, as is often believed, but the absence of deterrence.

That situation — the nullification of deterrence through double deterrence — could only be changed if deterrence was once again made one-sided: that is, if either side became able to threaten the other, without being threatened in return. This could come about in one of two ways.

The first is that one side might acquire the capacity to destroy all the nuclear weapons of its antagonist in one fell swoop, so that it need no longer fear retaliation. But this is in practice (even if such an assault were not a particularly inconceivable action) no longer a feasible option. Each side has been determined, above all else, to prevent that danger by ensuring that at least a part of its nuclear armoury would remain invulnerable. Each has ensured, therefore, by the number and variety of its nuclear warheads, and by holding them in clearly survivable forms — in hardened missile silos, in mobile missiles, in nuclear submarines, or on aircraft on permanent alert — that the hope that all could be eliminated in a single strike could not be realised. The possibility of a successful first strike is thus eliminated, since it must bring immediate retaliation in kind. This policy of "mutually assured destruction", though much derided, has in fact been followed by both alliances, and provides a more reliable assurance against the use of nuclear

nuclear response resulting from the number of "fingers on the trigger". It does not therefore necessarily portray the true position, and it can be taken as certain that at least those governments which have nuclear weapons on their territory have ensured that those weapons cannot be used without their consent.

weapons by the opponent than any known alternative.

The second method would be to improve counter-missile defences to such an extent that one side had a total assurance that, though its own nuclear weapons remained safe and could still do unacceptable damage to the enemy, the reverse was no longer the case. It could destroy the nuclear weapons available to the other side, while assured of a safe defence against retaliation.

This is the apparent objective of President Reagan's Strategic Defence Initiative (SDI), which aims to provide a sure defence against nuclear weapons. There are, however, many and easily recognisable deficiencies in that programme. The complicated system of satellites and lasers on which it depends does not, for example, even purport to be able to guard against missiles launched just offshore from submarines or ships; nor against low-flying Cruise-type missiles, which avoid detection on radar screens. The satellites on which the system depends are themselves vulnerable to attack (and the Soviet Union is highly advanced in anti-satellite warfare). The laser weapons intended to be used are so far highly unreliable. The computer programmes required would be infinitely more complex than any so far devised. Even among intercontinental weapons, the system is likely, if perfected, to give assurance of shooting down only a proportion — not, as is necessary, 100 per cent — of missiles fired. Above all, the programme is self-defeating, since, the closer it comes to success, the more surely it will stimulate the development of new offensive weapons, including, for example, more sophisticated decoys, which will overcome whatever advances may be made.

There is thus very little likelihood that the reality of mutual nuclear deterrence (which means mutual non-deterrence of conventional attacks) will be overcome by this means. But meanwhile vast sums will be spent by both sides in developing or combating a system which will not increase security for anyone. Even if the objective of the system were reduced to that of defending existing US missile sites, most of the objections would remain. It could never be made 100 per cent reliable for that purpose, as would be necessary; nor would it provide protection against submarine-based missiles fired from relatively short range, so that the development of these would be promoted.

But the fact that a strategic defence system is unlikely to work may not prevent it from being constructed. If it is, it will be severely damaging to international stability. It would extend the arms race into space, an area which the entire international community has sought to insulate from military uses, as in the Outer Space Treaty of 1967 (in 1962 the United States explicitly declared that it would not send nuclear weapons into space, yet the X-ray laser, an integral feature of the SDI, depends on the use of a nuclear explosion in space). Still more damagingly, however, the SDI, if finally deployed, would violate, and so bring to an end, the most significant arms-control agreement now in force: the Anti-Ballistic Missile (ABM) Treaty. That treaty reflected a recognition that strategic stability depended on the willingness of each side to allow the other to retain a second-strike capability, so deterring any first-strike by either side. Abrogation of this treaty would not only undo the restraint, which has been successfully imposed over 15 years, on the further development of anti-ballistic weapons, but destroy the existing nuclear balance by allowing one side to acquire at least the appearance of strategic invulnerability, and so a first-strike capacity. In that situation the Soviet Union would be expected to rely on a US undertaking that it would never exploit its new invulnerability to its own advantage: the kind of assurance the United States itself would certainly not be prepared to rely on if the position was reversed. The defensive nature of the system could only be guaranteed if the United States were willing, in siting its anti-missile defence, to abandon its own offensive missiles: something the US administration has never undertaken to do. Finally, more generally, the abandonment of a mutually agreed arms-control agreement would cast doubt on the durability of all future agreements, and so seriously damage stability and mutual confidence.

But the SDI, if put into effect, would cause another kind of instability. Whether or not a defensive shield could provide any security against nuclear attack for the United States, it is quite certain that it could not do so for Western Europe. While a system designed for the United States would be seeking to identify, track and shoot down missiles having a journey time of several minutes, the corresponding times for the short-range missiles targeted at Europe could be measured in seconds. Even the most enthusiastic supporters of the system do not maintain that the system could effectively nullify that threat. European security would therefore not be enhanced, but would actually be reduced, by SDI. The decoupling of European defence from that of the United States, which such moves as the introduction of intermediate missiles were designed to prevent, would be increased once more. And, by creating at least the appearance that the United States might survive a nuclear attack, the system would make that country appear less likely to regard the defence of Europe as essential to its own security. In consequence the capacity of the Soviet Union to dominate, and if necessary blackmail, Western Europe, through her nuclear and conventional superiority in that continent, would be increased.

It is for these reasons that most European leaders, together with many influential US observers (including several former Secretaries of State for Defence) are opposed to the SDI. In particular they attach great importance to the maintenance of the ABM treaty, so preserving mutual vulnerability and the existing nuclear balance. On the face of it, that treaty, which prohibits the testing, development and deployment of space weapons, might be thought to prohibit even some of the developments of the system already undertaken (among them demonstrations of missile intervention, which would appear closer to "testing" than "research"). Only controversial interpretation of these clauses — asserting that such activities represent only "research", required to match similar research undertaken in the Soviet Union — have allowed them to be presented as consistent with the treaty. If such differences are not to lead to the progressive erosion of the treaty terms, there is a need for new efforts to establish firmer definitions, so as to draw a clear line between "research", which is permitted under the treaty, and "testing" and "development", which are not. European governments, which, for the reasons given above, have a strong interest in the question, may have an important role in assisting that process, as well as in continuing to oppose the development of anti-missile defences which are so contrary to their interests.

Given the hideous destructive power of nuclear weapons, there is an obvious attraction in any system that might appear to provide a cast-iron defence against them. To rely rather on the threat of mutual assured destruction appears paradoxical and dangerous. But this is in fact a far more reliable source of security than the attempt to construct defences which, even if they could be made to work (which the vast majority of scientists on both sides of the Atlantic deny), can guard only against land-based missiles; which will destroy the symmetry of the existing balance; and which will damage confidence in the durability of any other arms-control measures which may be agreed. Continuance with such projects will involve the expenditure of many millions of dollars, which could be spent far better on other things. That expenditure would, moreover, be undertaken to guard against a form of attack which is increasingly inconceivable. It is thus hard to imagine a more irrational form of defence policy for Western countries to adopt.

Can the nuclear race be halted?

If nuclear weapons represent an unusable capacity, it not only becomes a pointless extravagance to attempt to develop expensive space-based defences against them: it is also senseless to continue to expend vast sums in developing ever more powerful and sophisticated nuclear warheads and means of delivery (see Table 2 for estimates of the East–West balance in 1986). So long as each side retains the capacity to deliver unacceptable damage to its opponent, it has the means to deter any threat to use nuclear weapons — however improbable — that might otherwise be made. So long as both sides retain that capability, they have no need to waste precious resources on expanding, or "modernising", what they already have. Thousands of millions of dollars could be saved which would be far better spent on more worthwhile purposes; and which, even if retained for defence, could more profitably be expended on the conventional deterrence which the declining

TABLE 2   THE EAST–WEST BALANCE: PRINCIPAL STRATEGIC
SYSTEMS, 1986

	East		*West*	
	Launchers	*Warheads*	*Launchers*	*Warheads*
Land-based	450 SS11	600–1140	450 Minutemen I	480
	150 SS17	630–1200	550 Minutemen II	1825
	300 SS18	3200–6200	17 (Titan) II	25
	360 SS19	2300–4300		
	45 SS25	47–90		
	(mobile)			
TOTAL	1305	6777–12,930	917	2330
Sea-based	40 SSN5	41–47	288 Poseidon	3300
	300 SSN6	480–550	360 Trident I	3200
	300 SSN8	310–350		
	224 SSN18	710–1900		
	80 SSN20	500–860		
	32 SSN23	240–270		
TOTAL	976	2281–3977	648	6500
Air-launched	20–30 Bison	36–130	263 B42	4733
	90 Bear	240–480	61 F111	360
	40 Bear H	160–320		
TOTAL	150–160	440–930	324	5093

Source: Stockholm International Peace Research Institute, *Arms and Disarmament* (Oxford, 1986).

credibility of nuclear weapons makes more than ever necessary.

The obvious way of reducing such valueless expenditure would be by securing agreement on measures of nuclear disarmament. The two SALT (Strategic Arms Limitation) agreements represent understandings which, if they did not bring any significant *reduction* in existing capabilities, did seek to impose maxima, in terms of launchers and warheads, and so to establish a measure of equilibrium (though even those understandings appear at the present time, with the US administration's announced intention of exceeding the SALT II limitations, on the point of collapse). An agreement covering the intermediate missiles, while having little effect on security (given the vast array of weapons which would remain), might also increase mutual confidence.

But it would be rash to place much hope in the likelihood of securing progress through agreements of this kind. The difficulties in arriving at durable agreements are well known. There are, first, considerable problems in matching different *kinds* of capability: in balancing, for example, the heavy land-based missiles favoured by the Soviet Union against the long-range bombers, capable of reaching Soviet territory, favoured by the United States; multiple-warhead intermediate missiles such as the Soviet SS20 against single-warhead but much more accurate missiles such as the US Pershing II; Soviet missiles at present deployed against China, but capable of being moved to the West, against US missiles targeted on the Soviet Union alone; US aircraft at present based in the United States, but capable of being transferred to Europe, against Soviet aircraft already based in Eastern Europe (or Soviet aircraft capable of reaching European targets but not capable of reaching the United States); ballistic missiles against non-ballistic missiles (such as Cruise); air-launched missiles against sea-launched missiles; "tactical" or "battlefield" nuclear weapons against conventional armaments. How many of one type should be reckoned as equivalent to how many of another? Even if agreement on numbers could be reached, there is room for wide disagreement about *qualitative* differences: for example, the relative accuracy of different missiles; their penetrative power; above all, their relative invulnerability. Finally, there are even more formidable problems in verifying compliance. Soviet leaders today are, happily, less hostile to verification measures than in the past. But no system of verification, even if it could be agreed, could be foolproof. While reasonable assurance might be secured concerning the numbers of intercontinental missiles, aircraft and warships held by either side (since these bulky objects could probably be detected by satellites or other means of physical inspection), there is no conceivable system which could give an absolute assurance that no *warheads* remained concealed, perhaps underground, somewhere in the vast expanses of the two countries; and there are almost equal difficulties in detecting relatively small, non-ballistic missiles, such as Cruise. Because of these difficulties, no matter how much effort is devoted to such negotiations, there is absolutely no possibility of an agreement which could provide assurance of the total destruction of the nuclear capability of either side. In other words, the whole 40-year search for measures to bring about the *elimination* of nuclear weapons has been devoted to a wholly impracticable ambition: a mirage, seductive but unattainable.

More limited measures, on the other hand, will have little effect. An agreement for the mutual withdrawal of intermediate missiles from Europe, for example, will do nothing to increase stability within the continent. It will not have the damaging consequences that some of its critics, especially in Europe, have alleged. It will not reduce the West's capacity to deter against nuclear attack, still less bring about the "denuclearisation" of Europe: on the contrary, it will remove only an insignificant fraction of the total number of nuclear warheads at present in Europe, leaving over 4000 on either side (as well as four times that number of strategic weapons outside the continent). It will not leave a gap in the spectrum of deterrence: a whole range of intermediate weapons, including US F111s, US submarine-based Cruise missiles, and US, British and French submarine-based ballistic missiles, will remain. The strategy of "flexible response" will therefore not be affected (which is to say it will remain as incredible as before). However, such an agreement will also not have the beneficial consequences which others have claimed for it. Since the number of nuclear weapons held by both sides will not be significantly reduced, security will not be enhanced. The danger presented by battlefield weapons will be unaffected. The West's reliance on a threat to reply with nuclear weapons to a conventional attack will remain as ineffective (because as incredible) as before. Above all, the kinds of weapons actually used in modern war — conventional weapons — will be entirely untouched, including any imbalance which may exist between East and West in such weapons.

The only kind of nuclear disarmament agreement which might significantly enhance security is of an entirely different kind. This would be one under which both sides undertook to abandon all land-based weapons (with the possible exception of mobile inter-continental weapons) in favour of much safer (because less vulnerable) sea-based weapons. Under such an agreement each side would retain an ultimate deterrent, and so the capacity to prevent nuclear blackmail by the other side. Whatever deterrent value nuclear weapons still have against conventional attack would be marginally increased, since it would no longer rely on the use of an unbelievable threat to end all civilised existence, in Germany and other front-line states. Some weapons at the intermediate level of the spectrum would be retained, in the form of submarine-based Cruise missiles. And the inherent instability caused by the plethora of existing weapons, especially short-range battlefield weapons, would be eliminated. Such an agreement would thus hugely improve the stability of the East–West balance and the credibility of the West's nuclear strategy. Unfortunately, however, given the opposition of the military to even modest changes in existing deployments, the chances of any such radical alteration in policy being adopted cannot be regarded as strong.

Because of the difficulty in ensuring verified reductions in nuclear weapons, there has been increasing interest in recent years in less ambitious measures. A powerful movement of opinion has developed, both in the United States and in Europe, demanding at least a "freeze" in the development and deployment of nuclear armaments. Since both sides now possess sufficient warheads to destroy the world many times over, there can, it is argued, be no possible purpose in developing ever more such weapons. Since both sides already hold their weapons in invulnerable, "survivable" forms, each already has the assurance of being able to inflict unacceptable damage on the other. Since, it is generally agreed, something like a parity in overall destructive power exists, neither side need object to a freeze on the grounds that it needs to "catch up" with the other in one field or another. Even, therefore, if it is impossible to agree on *formal* disarmament measures, at least each side could be expected to forgo any expansion of its existing capabilities and so to "freeze" the existing balance of nuclear power.

One might think that, given the vast cost of each new generation of nuclear weapons, and given the capacity of even existing systems to perform the only essential task (to be able to reach enemy targets), major governments would welcome such proposals with open arms. On the face of it, any measure that would have the effect of reducing defence expenditure, or at least enable it to be allocated more rationally, without damaging stability, has great attractions. It must, however, be recognised that there are real difficulties surrounding such proposals which need to be confronted. Some of them are similar to those which face disarmament agreements. And they cannot be summarily dismissed.

First, at what moment would the freeze begin? An essential premise of the proposal is that the principal parties accept that there already exists something like a "balance", and are therefore willing to live with this, rather than perpetually seek some further enhancement of their existing capabilities (often thus stimulating a corresponding effort to match this by their opponents). But at most times one side or the other, and occasionally both, believes that there is a need to redress a deficiency in one field or another — in miniaturisation of warheads, accuracy, hardening of missile sites, anti-satellite warfare, anti-submarine warfare, strategic defence, laser systems, and so on — if a balance is to be maintained. Each side fears, and so magnifies, the advantage it believes to have been gained by the other. Deciding the precise moment when parity has been reached and a freeze can be inaugurated is thus difficult enough even if there are only two parties to be considered. But, in fact, there are more than two. The difficulty of establishing the moment when the freeze begins applies particularly to minor nuclear powers, such as France, Britain and China; and, even more, to half a dozen near-nuclear states. If these are engaged in the last stages of upgrading their nuclear capability, or finally establishing themselves as nuclear-weapon nations, it is unlikely that they will suddenly agree to abandon that endeavour in the interests of bringing about a universal freeze. But *without* their agreement it is doubtful that the super-powers themselves could agree on a freeze. Could the Soviet Union, for example, be expected to cease improving its own nuclear capability if Britain and France (though not the United States) were allowed to continue to "modernise" theirs? And so on.

This raises a second question. Between whom is the freeze to be established? It is usually envisaged as a bilateral agreement between the two super-powers, or between the two alliances to which they belong (though the difference between the two could be crucial, as the example just given demonstrates). But, in this case, what would be the position of China? Would it also be expected to participate? And, if it did not, would the Soviet Union be willing to accept a measure that allowed a potential enemy to develop and improve its nuclear armoury? And, if China was invited to take part, should not India also be involved, on the grounds that an increase in its nuclear capability would alter the balance between itself and China? And would India agree to be involved without Pakistan, already a near-nuclear power? As these examples show, an agreed freeze between the super-powers alone is unlikely to be durable. What is required is a freeze agreed on a global basis: a balance which, given that it is not symmetrical, could prove exceedingly difficult to find.

Thirdly, does the concept of a freeze mean simply that no *new* missiles or means of delivery should be added to existing stocks; or does it mean that no alteration of any kind should be made, even to existing ones; in other words, that no "modernisation" should take place? At present such systems undergo a continuous process of redesign and replacement. If a freeze were accepted, would every weapon and every component part have to remain frozen precisely in its present form? As component parts wore out, or weapons aged, would they have to be replaced with others of exactly equivalent design, or even of equal age? Are land-based launchers never to be replaced by (safer) submarine launchers? And, if each side is to be permitted to maintain only its existing capability, who is to decide what form of replacement represents equivalence, and what type could enhance capability?

These are not inconsiderable difficulties in the way of any formal agreement for a freeze. But the difficulty in securing formal agreements does not mean that no restraints at all can be introduced. Restraint however is more likely to come about by unilateral measures than by formal understandings. Arms-control measures can be instituted without any formal treaty, and even without any explicit understanding. They can result from the deliberate policy decisions of each state, seeking to bring about a gradual transformation of the strategic equation: to change an accelerating arms race into a decelerating one, to exchange balance at a high level for balance at a low level, to replace weapon-procurement and strategic policies that appear threatening by policies that are manifestly defensive only.

Unilateral measures, therefore, have a role to play in bringing about a reduction in the level of nuclear armaments. It is unfortunate that the demand for unilateral disarmament over recent years has become indelibly associated with the demand for unilateral measures by individual states, in particular by Britain, for the abandonment of nuclear arms. Adherents of that movement, condemning nuclear weapons as "immoral", but apparently mainly fearful that their deployment may submit their countries to unacceptable risks (possibly the reason why there was no significant unilateralist movement in Britain while Britain itself was developing such weapons, but only when it became a potential target of Soviet weapons), have argued that, whatever the principal nuclear powers might do, at least their own states should rid themselves of nuclear weapons. By doing so, they claim, they would present a good example to other aspiring nuclear powers and cease to tempt them to unrealistic and dangerous ambitions. Such a step, it is recognised, would not significantly alter the overall nuclear balance between East and West. But it would at least ensure that their own states ceased to be an automatic target for annihilation in the first stages of a nuclear conflict.

The governments of Britain and France have so far shown no inclination to be influenced by such arguments. They point out that the cost of their nuclear forces represents only an insignificant fraction of their total defence budgets,* and the cost therefore does not prevent their making an adequate contribution to conventional deterrence as well. Their example in re-

---

* The proportion is in fact far higher for France (30 per cent) than for Britain (about 5 per cent), since France seeks to create a complete triad of means of delivery, with multiple-warhead missiles, entirely from its own resources.

nouncing nuclear weapons, they believe, would be most unlikely to influence other aspiring nuclear states which have
good reasons of their own — usually particular enemies they
especially fear (the surrounding Arab states for Israel, Israel
for Egypt and Iraq, India for Pakistan, the African front-line
states for South Africa, and so on) — for requiring nuclear
weapons, which would not be affected by any action which
Britain and France might take. Their countries would not cease
to be endangered by the nuclear weapons of other states because they had surrendered their own, and might indeed be
more so. Above all, they argue that nuclear weapons represent
for them the ultimate safeguard of their countries' sovereignty
and independence. Having acquired that sort of security at
great expense, they could not be expected, they believe, to
abandon it so long as other states retain a nuclear capacity.

This final argument is of course one that could be put forward by any state that had the desire and the capability to
become a nuclear power: which is no longer, technically or
economically, a very difficult undertaking. If nuclear weapons
genuinely provided a unique form of security, it might be
expected that mose developed states — including other European powers and Japan — would have decided to acquire such
a capability. If they have not done so, it is presumably because
they are generally content with the degree of security that their
existing armaments, together with US strategic and local
weapons, afford, and perhaps do not relish the somewhat
dubious prestige which a nuclear capability provides.

If there is any good reason for retention of nuclear weapons
by Britain and France, it is quite different from the chauvinist
and self-serving arguments commonly employed. It could, for
example, more reasonably be maintained that, whether of not
it is in the interests of Britain and France *individually* that they
should retain nuclear weapons, these weapons do help to
promote stability between East and West as a whole. As has
been pointed out earlier, the willingness of future US administrations to risk US cities for the sake of resisting a threat
directed at European targets alone could reasonably be
doubted by a potential aggressor. In that situation, the existence of nuclear weapons under European control might serve

to give pause to a state seeking to exploit its apparent local superiority. Although European governments are unlikely to be any more willing than the United States to authorise the use of nuclear weapons against a purely conventional attack, at least the Soviet Union could not believe that it was in a position to dominate Europe because European countries possessed no nuclear retaliatory capability at all. The capacity to inflict mutually assured destruction would create some kind of balance between the Soviet Union and Western Europe as well as between the Soviet Union and the United States. If the United States at some future time, as a result of domestic political developments, were to reduce its commitment to Europe, or even retreat into a "fortress America" position, the maintenance of a European capability would become even more important. Finally, the self-confidence of West European states is enhanced, it can be argued, and a healthier relationship with the United States maintained, if Western Europe does not totally depend on US nuclear weapons for its security.

Such arguments clearly carry some weight. What they make clear, above all, however, is that nuclear strategy is a question to be decided not by individual states alone but by West European states acting together, or by NATO as a whole. Calls for Britain, acting independently, to abandon its remaining nuclear weapons (or to expel all US nuclear establishments from British soil) express a deplorably narrow, essentially nationalistic approach to a problem that is above all international, not national. The call for "unilateral" nuclear disarmament from Britain (or France, or Denmark or the Netherlands) implies an arrogant belief that the leaders of those states can (like their predecessors in earlier centuries) alone determine the security of their own people. But the security of West European populations today depends not on national but on international factors. Decisions which affect the nuclear weapons of an individual state, or those on its territory, without affecting those of the Soviet Union or the United States or other countries, are totally irrelevant to that nation's security. The only security which is significant today is international, not national, security; and it is of little more significance to talk of the defence policy of Britain alone than it is to talk of the defence policy of Bedfordshire or Berkshire or Berwickshire.

What the people of Britain and other West Europen nations need to be concerned about today, therefore, is not the defence policy of their own governments but that of the collective bodies to which their countries belong. It is reasonable for them to demand changes in the defensive posture adopted by NATO as a whole: for example, that it should change its strategy so as to reduce its reliance on nuclear weapons. It is much less sensible for them to believe that such changes can be brought about by the unilateral actions of individual states. It is particularly irrational to demand actions which principally affect *another* member of the alliance, undertaken without consultation with that or any other member. Few people in Britain today would believe that West Germany was behaving reponsibly if it were suddenly to demand the removal of all foreign forces from its soil. For it would be recognised that it was undertaking an action affecting not only its own security but that of its allies as well. For Britain to take a similar step would be equally irresponsible: the action of Little Englanders rather than of Europeans; of party politicians rather than national statesmen; of self-centred nationalists rather than broad-horizoned internationalists.

If it is no longer sensible for individual European states to seek to pursue unilateral defence policies, there is much to be said for a greater degree of consultation among West European countries on such questions. The recent revival of West European Union may be a first step in that direction, though it is arguable that all EEC countries which are members of NATO need to be involved (see p. 142 below). The strategic interests of Western Europe, as we have seen, are in many ways different from those of the United States. Yet Western Europe is at present able to exercise little influence on the decisions reached by the US administration on such matters — concerning, for example, SDI, the abandonment of SALT, or a new agreement on intermediate missiles — even though it is deeply affected by their outcome. This applies not only to decisions reached about the deployment of nuclear weapons by the US but to those of other nuclear states of the region. There is clearly a need for much closer consultation than takes place at present on such questions: on the procurement of new nuclear weapons; on their deployment and targeting; and on the general strategy to be adopted concerning their use. As a result of such discussions the British and French nuclear forces would in time increasingly be seen as elements in a Western European capability, rather than as purely national forces. Increasing consultation could lead in time to something like joint decision-making on the way the forces were used. Decisions on firing could not be shared, since ultimately there could be only one finger on the trigger. But continuous collective discussion might ensure that those decisions were in practice governed by guidelines which had been collectively agreed.

Western Europe would then be in a position to contribute more effectively to the dialogue on defence questions, including disarmament, between the main alliances. It is East–West dialogue on such questions which is needed above all. For, though there are difficulties in bringing about *explicit* agreements on arms control, by continuous contacts and discussions it may be possible to secure better understanding of the common interest of both sides in restraint in the development and deployment of nuclear arms. Exchanges of view could take place about the advantages of alternative weapons systems (for example, sea-based as against more vulnerable land-based); about the advantages and disadvantages of strategic defence and forward defence; about systems of command, control and communication; above all, about crisis management and crisis prevention. It is through such a dialogue above all that the dangers of nuclear war — if any still exist — can be reduced to a minimum.

It may be that, in time, given the increasing implausibility that nuclear weapons could ever be brought into use, discussion of the strategy that should govern them, both within the alliances and between them, will appear less important. Such weapons may pass into the background, and come to be seen, like bacteriological weapons, nerve gases and other more horrific types of armament now available, as doomsday weapons which, though they cannot be disinvented or, therefore, abolished altogether, are no longer to be seen as serious instruments of war. At that time attention may at last begin to turn to the weapons which are in fact employed in the contemporary world; which are capable of inflicting increasingly devastating destruction; which could be called into use at any time, even in the relatively stable situation which exists in the European continent; and which therefore urgently need to be made the principal subject of disarmament negotiations at the present time.

The forgotten dimension

It is a strange paradox that it is the weapons of everyday use which have become today the forgotten dimension. During the 40-odd years since the Second World War, there have been few moments when conventional war, of larger or smaller proportions, has not been in progress in one part of the world or another. In the Korean War, in the Arab–Israeli wars, the wars in Vietnam and Afghanistan, and the hundred or so other conflicts which have taken place during that time, it has been "conventional" weapons, not nuclear, which have been employed. It is with such weapons that over 20 million people have lost their lives in war since 1945. Yet for over 40 years the attention of all statesmen, military leaders and commentators, has been focused overwhelmingly not on the weapons which have been used but on those which have not, and which, many believe, are now unusable. Vast sums continue to be spent in building up ever-larger stocks of weapons which are too powerful to use. Even the deterrent value of such weapons is limited, since they are only able to deter an attack with similar weapons: of a kind, in other words, which nobody seriously believes is now conceivable. They are no longer able, as we have seen, to deter the only type of war that is still credible: one that is intended from the beginning to be conducted only with conventional weapons. Yet in discussions of defence policy within states and in negotiations on disarmament questions between states alike, attention continues to be focused almost entirely on this obsolete type of weaponry.*

* It is symptomatic of this neglect that the text of the following pages is taken, with only minor alterations, from an article on conventional disarmament first published over 20 years ago.

This neglect of the conventional component can scarcely be because conventional weapons are innocuous, and can therefore be safely ignored. There is no more alarming misconception than the widespread belief that, while the terrors of nuclear war are such as to threaten the future of mankind, the dangers of conventional war could fairly easily be tolerated. "Conventional" war is habitually identified with war that is not too horrific. Its associations are with the type of conflict that the world endured, and survived, in 1939–45, or with the limited conflicts of recent years. This assumption is a highly dangerous one. Even the Second World War, with the relatively primitive "conventional" military technology then available, caused something like 50 million deaths and destruction on a scale never before imagined. Even then it was said that the continued use of V2s against London for another six months would have made that city uninhabitable. Even then, "conventional" bombing raids on Tokyo and Dresden caused, in a single night, more casualties than raids with atomic weapons a few months later. Today, with the types of missile, guidance mechanism, and explosive power now readily available, even a war restricted to conventional weapons would make the horrors of the last conflagration appear trifling in comparison.

Modern missiles, saturation bombing, rocket artillery, submarine rockets, "smart" weapons of various kinds, guidance mechanisms of increasingly sophisticated types, anti-personnel mines, cluster bombs, particle beam and kinetic energy weapons, lasers, dioxin, napalm and other chemical weapons designed to burn their victims alive — these and others less well known or still being devised could wreak damage, both on troops and civilian populations, that was infinitely more devastating than any inflicted in previous conflicts. It is impossible to know what further refinements contemporary technology may now be devising, still less what it may soon provide. The very word "conventional", in the accepted sense of non-nuclear, is thus a totally misleading one. Many non-nuclear weapons today are very far from conventional, and are hugely destructive. In other words, the same technological progress which has produced nuclear weapons, with all their horror, has also made conventional weapons far more destructive than ever before.

At the same time the distinction between military and civilian targets, already largely abandoned in the Second World War, has become still further blurred. There is every likelihood, therefore, that a major conflict confined to "conventional" weapons would prove (as several recent wars — Vietnam and the Gulf War, for example — have suggested) far more lethal than any war of earlier times.

It is somewhat strange in these circumstances that so little of the attention lavished on disarmament questions in recent times has been devoted to the means of limiting and, if possible, reducing the levels or the destructive capabilities of such weapons. Yet it is reductions in this area alone which will affect the type of arms ever actually employed in war. And, for that reason, it is reductions in this area which would be of greatest value in increasing mutual confidence. Above all, it is agreement in this area that would do most to establish a balance between East and West, since it is in this area that the imbalances are generally believed to be greatest.

There is thus every advantage in seeking to secure conventional disarmament, regardless of any imbalances that are believed to remain in the field of nuclear armaments. Many of the difficulties that have traditionally prevented agreements on disarmament are far less if they are focused on conventional weapons. Apprehensions concerning national security, which are inevitably aroused in their extreme form by negotiations aiming at nuclear disarmament, are unlikely to prove so formidable in the case of negotiations concentrated on conventional weapons alone. While the undetected retention of a handful of hydrogen bombs could be crucial in destroying the balance established by disarmament, the possible retention of a hundred extra tanks could scarcely be vital to a conventional agreement. Since no concession could deprive either side of the ultimate deterrent, or represent a final sacrifice of sovereignty or security, there may be a greater willingness to arrive at limited agreements in this sphere, which could none the less mark an important step forward. Furthermore, with conventional weapons the problems of establishing a balance in different types of armament are reduced, and the difficulties of inducing lesser nuclear powers, such as Britain, France and

China, and potential nuclear powers, to accept restraints are bypassed.

When conventional disarmament is considered in isolation, the problem of verification is also less contentious. For the establishment of an inspection system covering conventional weapons need not demand a total surrender of sovereignty or security. The setting-up of control posts, the institution of air-inspection and similar measures should be sufficient to retain some check on conventional capacity, at least in the early stages, without the type of intrusive inspection of industrial and other installations, the questioning of citizens, or the other detailed verification measures which the Soviet Union has traditionally resisted. Adequate verification, in other words, could probably be secured by the type of control measures that are now acceptable to all parties.

It is particularly surprising that Western states have not done more to focus interest on conventional disarmament. It is they that continually complain of Soviet superiority in the conventional field, and cite it as the reason why they still feel it necessary to threaten the use of nuclear weapons even against a purely conventional attack. And it is they, therefore, that, because that threat — with nuclear stalemate — has now become less plausible, have the greatest interest in measures which might establish some kind of parity in conventional forces alone.

A parity in conventional armaments can be secured in one of two ways. One would be by a substantial increase in the existing conventional forces of the West. The degree of imbalance which exists at present is disputed, depending as it does on calculations of the *quality* of Eastern-bloc forces and equipment, as well as their numbers. The Soviet bloc undoubtedly has a superiority in tanks and fighter aircraft. But this is offset by a superiority on the Western side in anti-tank weapons and interdiction aircraft. The balance in hardware is, anyway, not decisive, given the West's believed superiority in many qualitative dimensions, including electronic warfare, precision and guided missiles, surveillance and command, communication and control.* A recent report to Congress by the US Under-Secretary of Defense for Research and Engineering concluded that in the 20 most important basic technology areas, the US was superior in 15, equal in four and behind only in one. The overall superiority of the Warsaw Pact forces has been reckoned as about 1.2:1, a level far too small to provide sufficient advantage to an attacking side. It is conventionally calculated that an attacking force would need a 3:1 advantage to be sure of securing success; and, if this ratio is accepted, even the current level of the West's conventional forces would be adequate.* If the three nuclear powers within the alliance were adequate.† rather larger proportion of their defence budgets to conventional arms, or if the other member states were to increase their total military budgets by only a small amount, the imbalance would already be significantly reduced. The combined gross national products of the 16 members of NATO is about three times that of the Warsaw Pact powers; and, given more rapid rates of growth in the West, that imbalance is probably now increasing rather than declining. Whatever the imbalance which exists at present, therefore, it should be perfectly possible for the members of NATO to match the Warsaw Pact forces in conventional arms. This is all the more apparent

---

* Qualitative differences of this kind have made nonsense of comparisons in purely numerical terms. The number of tanks held by East and West, for example, is often compared without reference to the fact that the average firing rate of Western tanks is double that of Soviet tanks; comparisons are made of numbers of aircraft, without reference to their differing ranges, manoeuvrability and, above all, electronic aids, which in modern conditions (as Israeli successes against Syria have shown) are often decisive.

† The International Institute of Strategic Studies, estimating the balance in conventional forces between NATO and the Warsaw Pact in Europe, concludes (in *The Military Balance 1986–7*) that "The conventional balance is still such as to make general military aggression a highly risky undertaking for either side. ... There would still appear to be insufficient overall strength on either side to guarantee victory."

when account is taken of the Soviet Union's need to cover its flank against China, and the possible unreliability of some East European forces.

But, if there continues to be doubt about the West's ability to match the Soviet Union's conventional forces, the alternative, and preferable, way to bring about parity would be by securing a disarmament agreement covering such weapons. This could bring about the desired goal without the exertion and cost of increased military spending. Until now little real energy or enthusiasm has been devoted to negotiations of this type. It is true that discussions on "mutual balance force reductions" (MBFR) have been proceeding in a desultory fashion for a decade and a half. But these have never got beyond the stage of futile argument about the precise level of the forces already deployed in particular areas. The area where the reductions would take place is narrowly defined (omitting, for example, Hungary and most of European Russia), and no account is taken of Soviet forces in other parts of Russia or of US forces in the United States, so that the value of any agreement would, anyway, be highly marginal. There has been little serious discussion about the numbers of tanks, aircraft and other weapons which would be permitted to each state within the area to bring about a greater symmetry; what allowance would be made, if any, for Soviet defence requirements in Asia; the measures of verification that would be needed to make disarmament in this field a reality; and other fundamental questions that would need to be considered if a balance was to be achieved. Still less has there been discussion on wider but arguably more important questions: the adoption of appropriate *strategies* and *procurement policies*, defensive rather than offensive, to reduce future threats; and the type of command, control and communications systems (between alliances as well as within them) that would best help to reduce dangers in a crisis. The agreements which have been arrived at in this field, concerning the notification of military manoeuvres — measures which would, anyway, be immediately rescinded at a time of serious crisis — are entirely insignificant in relation to the benefits which might be had through more intensive and systematic negotiations on such questions.

Conventional disarmament has therefore become of triple importance. By securing some kind of balance in conventional forces it could lessen the risk of that type of conflict which now seems most likely to occur. By nullifying the existing Soviet preponderance in conventional forces, it could save the Western powers from having to engage in a level of conventional rearmament that might prove economically burdensome. And, by presenting a field in which a limited measure of international inspection, within a specified field, might prove acceptable, it could represent a first step towards disarmament agreements of other kinds. It is therefore surely time to switch our attention from the alluring possibility of agreements on reductions in nuclear weapons — agreements that would be very difficult if not impossible to secure, impossible to verify and relate to a type of weapon now increasingly obsolete — to agreements covering the weapons that are actually used by states when making war.

It would be wrong to attach too much hope to the negotiation of agreements of this kind. The long history of such discussions does not provide much room for optimism. Though a few understandings have occasionally been reached (see Table 3), they have never provided for significant *reductions* in levels of armament. Where they have provided for restraints, it has always been at a high level, often higher than those previously reached; and, even then they have often, as in the case of the pre-war naval agreements and post-war SALT treaties, not proved enduring. They have in recent times been confined to nuclear weapons, which are not the weapons that are used in modern war, and even in that case have not prevented total stockpiles from steadily increasing (the total number of nuclear warheads in the world has now reached about 50,000). Even if reductions were to be agreed, and were extended to cover conventional armaments, the levels would still probably be above those actually used in the conflicts of the modern world. In other words even *successful* negotiations (for example, in MBFR) would not significantly restrain the ability of states to make war.

So long as major powers reserve to themselves the right to make use of armed force, where they think it necessary, to

TABLE 3   DISARMAMENT AND ARMS-CONTROL AGREEMENTS,
1921–86

Agreements	Date
Washington Naval Agreement	1921
(limiting capital ships of USA, UK, France, Italy and Japan)	
Geneva Protocol	1925
(banning of poison gas in war)	
London Naval Agreements	1930
(limiting naval tonnage of USA, UK and Japan)	
Demilitarisation of Antarctic	1959
Ban on nuclear testing except underground	1963
Communications ("hot line") link	1963
(USA and USSR)	
Reduction in production of fissionable materials	1964
(USA, USSR and UK)	
Treaty on Peaceful Use of Outer Space	1967
(banning orbiting of nuclear weapons and other weapons of mass destruction)	
Treaty on Latin American Nuclear-free Zone	1967
Non-Proliferation Treaty	1970
(prohibiting transfer of nuclear weapons by nuclear parties and acquisition of such weapons by non-nuclear parties to the treaty)	
Nuclear Accidents Agreements	1971,
(providing for immediate notification of an incident involving	1976,
a nuclear weapon or a detection of unidentified objects	1977
on radar screens; USA–USSR, France–USSR, UK–USSR)	
Sea-bed Treaty	1971
(banning emplacement of nuclear weapons on the sea-bed beyond 12 miles from shore)	
Biological Weapons Convention	1972
(banning biological warfare)	
ABM Treaty	1972
(limiting anti-ballistic missile systems)	
SALT I	1972
(setting ceilings on number of missile launchers; US and USSR)	
Prevention of Nuclear War	1973
(committing each party to act so as to prevent the outbreak of nuclear war and any threat or use of force)	
Helsinki Agreement	1975
(providing for notification of major military manoeuvres; extended 1986)	
Environment Modification Convention	1977
(prohibiting hostile use of techniques producing substantial environmental modifications)	
Protocol I, 1949 Geneva Convention	1977
(modernising rules of war to relieve suffering of civilians and damage to dams, dykes and nuclear power stations)	
Protocol II, 1949 Geneva Convention	1977
(laying down rules of war in civil conflicts)	

Agreements	Date
SALT II (unratified) (setting ceilings on nuclear launchers and bombers, including sub-limits for particular categories, and on numbers of warheads)	
Inhumane Weapons Convention (restricting use of fragmentation weapons, mines, booby traps and incendiary weapons)	1981

protect their interests, there will be a limit to their willingness to accept substantial reductions in armaments. They are unlikely to be ready to reduce them to a level below those that they have actually used — for example, in Afghanistan or Vietnam. And, even if they were to do so, such agreements would probably be repudiated as soon as any crisis arose which made rearmament appear essential to national interests. Disarmament may be of help in increasing mutual confidence. But it is not a means of preventing war.

It is not so much on the number of arms that are held on either side, but on the way they are used, that negotiation is most necessary. It is on national *behaviour,* not national capabilities, that understandings are required today. And it is to the possibility of understandings of that kind that our attention must now be directed.

3   The Localisation of War

An observer in 1945, looking back over the evolution of warfare during the previous few centuries, would have been impressed with the relentless increase in its scale and destructiveness. He would have noted the consistent increase in the lethal power of the weapons employed: from sword, lance, bow and arrow in the Middle Ages, through gunpowder, musket and cannon in the sixteenth and seventeenth centuries, to increasingly powerful artillery, mines and naval warships two centuries later, followed by machine guns, tanks, submarines and aircraft in the First World War, and culminating in the unprecedented destructiveness of guided missiles and atomic bombs only 20 years later. He would have seen the progressive increase in the size of armies employed. He would have observed the growth in the numbers of casualties: from tens of thousands in many wars of the late Middle Ages to hundreds of thousands in the nineteenth century, 10–12 million in the First World War, and an estimated 40–50 million in the Second World War. He would have noted the increase in the number of states involved in an average war, from two or three in the fifteenth and sixteenth centuries to six or ten in the eighteenth century, to 30 in the First World War and over 40 in the Second; with a corresponding increase in the geographical extent of the areas covered, growing steadily to reach the world-wide scale of the Second World War (perhaps the only genuine "world war" in history). And such an observer would perhaps have asked himself, with trepidation, if this progressive increase in the scale of war, and of its casualties, was likely to continue, equally inexorably, in the years to come.

Looking back 40 years later, the same observer might have been both depressed and encouraged. He would have been depressed by the fact that war had been no less favoured than

57

before as an instrument of state policy. Indeed, it had become, if anything, more common: betweem 1945 and 1986, about 120 significant wars had been fought.* Many of these had been substantial conflicts, involving very many casualties: something approaching 2 million deaths are thought to have occurred in the Korean War, a similar number in the wars in Indo-China, and over 250,000 in at least eight others. Many had been fought with great ferocity, and with less concern to limit casualties and suffering than in many earlier times. A number had continued for 15 years or more. Nor was there any indication that the propensity for war was declining. 40 years after 1945, 20 wars, of varying degrees of intensity, were taking place in different parts of the world (p. 169 below). Total casualties during those 40 years have been estimated (in a United Nations study) at 20–5 million: not as great as during the Second World War, but almost certainly much higher than in any similar period before 1914.

On the other hand, the observer would have noticed that no war had taken place of the kind that had most been feared in 1945: an all-out war among the major powers of the world — not even one fought with "conventional" weapons only. Since the end of the Second World War, none of the weapons most feared at that time — nuclear, bacteriological or (on a significant scale) chemical — had been employed. Even more striking, most of the developed states of the world, he would have seen, had remained entirely free of war throughout this period — something unprecedented in any earlier time. No war at all had taken place in Europe during the previous 30 years: probably the longest period of peace the continent had known in recorded history.

Of course it was not totally impossible that war could take place among developed states once more. It was still conceivable that some local conflict in Europe could lead to a military confrontation between East and West. A revolution in an East European country, an incident in Berlin, an encroachment upon Austrian neutrality, a crisis in Greece or Turkey or some

---

* For statistics concerning wars in this period, see Luard, *War in International Society*, Appendices 4 and 5.

other country might lead to intervention by one or (far less probably) both sides. What was scarcely conceivable was that such a crisis could, in modern conditions, lead to an all-out total war between East and West; still less that there could occur, as widespread opinion seemed to assume, a sudden unprovoked assault by the forces of one side against the other. Such a conflict bore no relationship to the fundamental aims and interests of either side. On the contrary, both had every interest in avoiding it by every possible means. Were incidents to occur, therefore (as they did occur in Berlin in 1948–9 and 1959–61, and in Eastern Europe in 1956, 1968 and 1981), it was inconceivable that responses would not be as carefully limited, in terms of both the area affected and the level of weaponry involved, as at the time of each of these incidents — and, indeed, in all the other conflicts of the post-1945 world, both in Europe and elsewhere. "Flexible response" and "limited war" were the doctrines now generally recognised. Self-denying ordinances of that kind were in the manifest interests of all. Least of all did it seem possible, for the reasons described in the last chapter, that nuclear weapons could be employed if such a conflict were to break out.

There could be no certainty that this state of affairs would continue. But there were reasonable grounds for expecting it to do so. This was only partly because there existed a balance of power between East and West. All past experience shows that a balance of power has frequently failed to bring peace (in 1756, in 1870 and in 1914, to take only some obvious examples). Nor was the peace in Europe to be attributed to nuclear deterrence, which, as we have seen, can no longer deter conventional war. The really important factor was that no state of Europe appeared to have the least interest in a war within that continent. There were no major revisionist states, yearning for the opportunity for significant territorial acquisitions or adjustments of the balance of power in their favour, as had existed before 1939. Most of the states of the continent were integrated within stable alliances, which served to deter unilateral action, either within or between them. Clearly defined spheres of influence had become accepted, causing each side to refrain from intervening, even in incidents involving the use of force, within the sphere of its opponents (as in 1956 and 1968).

Even war *within* the devloped states of the world now seemed far less likely. The increasing centralisation of power meant that the balance of power between governments and potential rebel forces was so overwhelmingly in favour of the government that dissident forces had no prospect of success (perhaps the reason why dissent increasingly took the form of sporadic terrorism rather then civil war). Political systems, whether authoritarian or democratic, were increasingly stable and resistant to change. Finally, higher standards of living meant that populations were less and less inclined to undergo the hardships and privations which revolutionary struggles entailed. To a large extent in such societies the mentality necessary for war — anger at injustice sufficiently intense to motivate a willingness to undergo high risk and prolonged suffering — no longer existed.

Major international war among developed states therefore now seemed an increasingly improbable eventuality. The wars of the contemporary world, our observer would have seen, now took place almost without exception within and among developing countries. Among those countries most of the factors that made war unattractive in rich states did not obtain. Central government power was not sufficient to make rebellion a hopeless undertaking. Political systems were not stable. Oppression or injustice was extreme enough to drive significant numbers to seek to overcome it by violent means. And many groups and individuals were sufficiently desperate to make armed rebellion appear an attractive option for them.

But the fact that war now took place almost entirely within the developing world did not mean that developed states did not sometimes become heavily involved. Nor did the fact that most of the wars were local, within frontiers rather than across them, mean that they were necessarily small and insignificant. A signficant number were on a major scale, involving many casualties. Civil wars in China (1946–9), Colombia (1948–58), Sudan (1955–72), Nigeria (1967–9), Afghanistan (1978–) and Uganda (1980–) each took hundreds of thousands of lives. In a number of cases major powers became heavily involved. This applied especially to the super-powers. The Soviet Union undertook armed action in Hungary in 1956, in Czechoslovakia in 1968 and in Afghanistan from 1980 onwards; the United States was involved in actions in Vietnam and other parts of Indo-China in 1961–73, in the Dominican Republic in 1965, in Grenada in 1983 and in Lebanon in 1983–4, besides giving substantial assistance to military actions in Guatemala in 1954, Cuba in 1961 and Nicaragua from 1982 onwards. The apparent immunity of the developed world from war was thus something of an illusion. Such states did still sometimes become involved directly or indirectly. But they became involved not immediately against their main opponents, but in other countries, much less powerful than themselves, where they believed their own security interests to be at stake.

The fact that war had become localised did not therefore mean that it had become small in scale or in effect. Local wars could involve many casualties. They could be intense and prolonged. They could be decisive in their political effects on the countries where they occurred. And, for that reason, they often stimulated the large-scale involvement of other states, including some of the major states of the world.

The wars that occurred none the less fell into a number of quite different categories. And, before considering how the dangers they represent might be reduced, it may be worth seeking to distinguish more carefully between the different types of local war which have occurred in recent years.

Categories of conflict in the contemporary world

Altogether, in the period since 1945, there have been at least 127 significant wars.* Of that number, two took place in Europe; 26 in Latin America; 31 in Africa; 24 in the Middle East; and 44 in Asia.

---

* There are obvious problems of definition in establishing the figures. For these purposes a series of isolated terrorist acts or sporadic engagements are not defined as "wars". Nor are *coups d'état*, which are rapidly concluded, even if they involve heavy casualties. Nor are disorganised riots and other disturbances. For a discussion of these problems of definition and a listing of the wars, see Luard, *War in International Society*, pp. 5–7 and Appendix 5.

17 were colonial wars: that is, were undertaken by groups within colonial territories in order to secure a more rapid transition towards independence, or to ensure that the group which undertook them would be recognised as the authentic representatives of their people before independence (see Table 4). Such wars naturally took place especially in the territories where, for whatever reasons, the prospect of independence was withheld, permanently or temporarily: in Indonesia, where the Netherlands at first sought to re-establish colonial rule indefinitely; in Cyprus, where it was stated at one time that independence would "never" be granted; in Algeria, held to be a part of France itself and so never to be accorded, as were French territories in black Africa, the right of independence; in the Portuguese territories, also held to be (before the Portuguese revolution of 1974) a part of metropolitan Portugal and so not fit for decolonisation. Wars occurred also where effective power was held, as in the case of Rhodesia, by a white minority unwilling, whatever the metropolitan government might decide, to relinquish power to a black majority; or, as in the case of Namibia, where the colonial power would only

TABLE 4   PRINCIPAL COLONIAL CONFLICTS, 1945–86

Dates	Parties
1945–9	Netherlands – Indonesians
1946–54	Indo-Chinese – France
1947	France – Madagascans
1952–4	Tunisians – France
1952–7	Kenyans – Britain[a]
1953–6	Moroccans – France
1954–62	Algerians – France
1955–9	Cypriots – Britain[a]
1955–60	Camerounians – France
1957–8	West Saharans – France, Spain
1961–74	Angolans – Portugal
1961	India – Portugal (Goa)
1963–74	Guineans (Bissau) – Portugal
1963–7	South Arabia – Britain[a]
1965–74	Mozambicans – Portugal
1966–	Namibians – South Africa
1973–80	Rhodesians – Britain

[a] In these cases war took place between the peoples of the colonial territory as well as against the colonial power.

accord independence in a way which would effectively deny control to the majority party in the territory. This is a category of war which reflected the tensions of a particular period of history: when there was a substantial gap between the aspirations of the many peoples of colonial territories for independence and the willingness of their colonial masters to accord it to them, leading to conflict and often to war. Though such struggles aroused considerable sympathy elsewhere, they did not normally lead to active intervention. Today the territories still remaining under colonial rule are in general small territories where there is little or no demand for independence (and where occasionally indeed the colonial power has a greater desire to rid itself of colonial responsibilities than have the people of the territory themselves for such a change). Though occasionally there remain (as in New Caledonia) ethnic or other problems which could break out in armed warfare, on balance it is likely that conflicts of this kind will not now recur.

A number of wars since 1945 have occurred in the immediate *aftermath* of independence, as a result of dissatisfaction over the outcome. Several of these have been territorial disputes of one kind or another. Of this kind were, for example, the two wars between India and Pakistan over Kashmir (1949–50 and 1965); those fought by Indonesia over East Malaysia, West Irian and East Timor before or after the decolonisation of those territories; and the war between Algeria and Morocco in 1962. The four Arab–Israeli wars of 1948–9, 1956, 1967 and 1973 could be regarded as falling within this category, since all stemmed from a struggle for power after the ending of the British mandate in Palestine in 1948. In some cases wars have arisen as a result of *domestic* conflict, either before or after independence, arising from a struggle for power among contending groups: as in the Congo (1960–5), Aden (1966–7) and Nigeria (1967–9). (The very large number of coups and attempted coups in Africa in the 1960s were a lesser manifestation of the same phenomenon.) In general, wars in this category, like colonial wars, have stimulated few attempts at intervention from outside. They have usually been fought over issues of immediate concern only to those directly involved. And they too, as decolonisation recedes, will decline in significance (where such conflicts persist, as in Angola and Mozambique, they have become with time little different from the civil wars occurring in other developing countries).

Next, there have been a substantial number of frontier conflicts: border wars fought on a local basis, to win or maintain control of particular areas where a frontier was disputed or uncertain (see Table 5). Of this kind were, for example, the limited engagements between China and India in 1959–62; between China and the Soviet Union in 1969; between Ecuador and Peru in 1981; and between Mali and Burkina Fasso in 1985, among others. One or two more large-scale wars

TABLE 5   FRONTIER WARS, 1945–86[a]

Dates	States involved	Disputed territory
1947–9	Pakistan – India	Kashmir
1950–62	Afghanistan – Pakistan	Pushtu territories of N. Pakistan
1954–62	Cambodia – Thailand	Temple of Preah Vihar
1955	Abu Dhabi, Muscat – Saudi Arabia	Buraimi
1957	Nicaragua – Honduras	Coco river region
1958	Egypt – Sudan	Areas north of 22nd parallel
1959	India – China	Areas of Ladakh
1962	Morocco – Algeria	Tindouf
1962	China – India	India's N.E. frontier and Ladakh
1963–5	Indonesia – Malaysia	Malaysia's Borneo territories
1963–4	Dahomey – Niger	Lete island in river Niger
1963–7	Somalia – Kenya	Somali-inhabited territories of Kenya
1965	Pakistan – India	Rann of Kutch
1965	Pakistan – India	Kashmir
1969	China – Soviet Union	Amur boundary
1973–	Libya – Chad	Aouzov strip
1977–8 & sporadic	Somalia – Ethiopia	Ogaden
1978–9	Uganda – Tanzania	Kagera Salient
1980–	Iraq – Iran	Shatt-el-Arab boundary
1981	Ecuador – Peru	Cordillera del Condor
1982	Argentina – Britain	Falklands/Maldives
1985–6	Burkina Fasso – Mali	Agacher
Sporadic	Aden, South Yemen – Yemen	Various parts of the border

[a] The total number of *disputes* about frontiers is very much greater. This list includes only cases in which some type of armed action has taken place, even if short of full-scale war. The categories are not necessarily mutually exclusive: some conflicts fall into more than one category.

which were stimulated at least in part by a frontier conflict can be placed within this category: such as the war between Iran and Iraq beginning in 1980. Again there has in general been little intervention from outside in such wars. They have been seen as essentially bilateral conflicts not touching the vital interests of more distant powers.

But most of the wars of this period have belonged to none of these types. They have been civil wars, fought entirely within the frontiers of a single state. Of the 127 wars since 1945, 73 have been primarily civil wars, though in a number of them intervention from outside has subsequently occurred. If the 17 anti-colonial wars are included the number comes to 90: approaching three-quarters of the total.

A number of these have been rebellions by ethnic minorities, seeking to win independence, or at least autonomy, for their group. As Table 6 shows, there have been at least 24 wars in this category during the period, in addition to sustained campaigns confined to terrorist action (such as the campaigns

TABLE 6   MINORITY REVOLTS, 1945–86

Dates	State	Minority peoples
1948–	Burma	Karens, Kachens, Shans, etc.
1950	Indonesia	South Malaccans
1955–9	India	Nagas
1955–72, 1982–	Sudan	Southerners
1957–61	Indonesia	People of north Celebes, Sumatra
1959	China	Tibetans
1960–5	Congo	Katangans and others
1961–	Ethiopia	Eritreans
1961–75, 1980–	Iraq	Kurds
1963–4	Cyprus	Turkish speakers
1966–8	India	Mizos
1967–9	Nigeria	Ibos
1968–76	Oman	Dhofaris
1969–	Indonesia	West Papuans
1971–	Philippines	Moslems of the south
1972	Burundi	Hutus
1975–	Bangladesh	Chittagong hill tribes
1975–	Indonesia	East Timor
1975–	Ethiopia	Tigreans
1977–82	Ethiopia	Somalis
1979–8	Vietnam, Laos	Montagnards
1983–	Sri Lanka	Tamils

of the Basques in Spain, Corsicans in France, Catholic republicans in Northern Ireland, Sikhs in India, Armenians against
Turkey, Croats against Yugoslavia, and so on) not listed here
as wars. Prolonged struggles, lasting sometimes for decades,
have been fought by some minority peoples: for example, by
the Kurds against Iraq and Iran, by the Eritreans and Trigreans
against Ethiopia, by the Nagas and Mizos against India, and by
the West Saharans against Morocco. Sometimes, as in the case
of the religious sects in South Vietnam in 1955–6, or the
Moslems fighting in the southern Philippines, the minorities
have been distinguished by their religion, rather than by their
ethnic character. The most bitter and protracted struggles of all
have occurred where entire countries are divided on religous
and/or ethnic lines: for instance, Sudan, divided between Moslem and Arab north and Christian (or animist) and African
south; Chad, divided between Moslem north and Christian
south; and Lebanon, divided between factions representing
half-a-dozen religious sects as well as political and regional
groups. In these cases too, large-scale intervention has not
normally taken place, though in some cases arms have been
provided, or an adjoining country has afforded the rebels a
base (as Algeria has done for the West Saharans, and as Iran
has done at different times for Iraqi Kurds).

But the great majority of the civil wars have been political in
character. As we saw in Chapter 1, the dominant concern of
the current age, and the main source of conflict, is political
belief. Civil wars are therefore no longer fought mainly about
religious belief or claims to succession. Overwhelmingly they
are fought about which particular political faction shall rule.
As might be expected, such wars are less common in democratic countries, where it is harder to justify rebellion against a
government having majority support (and where there is less
reason to do so). They occur above all in authoritarian states
where the legitimacy of the governments may be challenged
and where frequently oppression, corruption and large-scale
inequalities occur. In a substantial number of cases (see Table
7) these wars can be called "ideological" in the conventional
sense: that is, they have been fought between factions proclaiming Communist or at least left-wing views against others

TABLE 7   IDEOLOGICAL CIVIL WARS, 1945–86

Dates	Country
1946–9	Greece
1946–54	Philippines
1948–53	Colombia
1946–50, 1954–6	China
1948–60	Malaya, Malaysia
1948	Costa Rica
1955–6	South Vietnam (religious groups)
1955	Costa Rica
1958	Lebanon
1959–62, 1963–75	Laos
1959–75	South Vietnam
1962–7	Yemen
1965–	Colombia
1965	Dominican Republic
1965–6	Indonesia
1965–6	Peru
1968–76	Oman
1970–5	Cambodia
1974–	Philippines
1975–9	Argentina
1975–	Lebanon
1976–	Angola
1976–	Guatemala
1978–9	Yemen
1979–	Afghanistan
1979–	El Salvador
1980–	Cambodia
1980–	Mozambique
1980–	Nicaragua
1981–	Peru

representing anti-Communist or conservative opinions. It is in these cases that intervention from outside has been most frequent, since the outcome of such struggles is often seen as of vital strategic importance to major external powers, including the super-powers. Typical of this kind have been the civil wars in China (1946–50), Greece (1944–5), Vietnam (1959–75), Nicaragua (1961–79), El Salvador (1980–), Angola (1975–) and Mozambique (1975–). In all of these the struggle was in the first place between local groups proclaiming conflicting political beliefs; and it is in such struggles above all that external intervention, to promote the victory of one or other faction, became most common.

These then are the main forms of war in the modern world. The most striking feature they have in common is that, however bitterly they are contested, whatever the scale of the fighting, however heavy the casualties, they are geographically confined. However many states may become involved, directly or indirectly, these wars have almost all taken place within the frontiers of a single state. There are no world wars; no wars involving one developed state against another; and few external wars, of state against state, at all. To a substantial extent wars are fought out within states; and in them factions of rival ideologies contest with each other, often supported and supplied, occasionally directly assisted, by their all-powerful patrons overseas.

The limits to localisation

At first sight, therefore, most wars in the modern world are highly localised.

Even where they occur between two different states (as, for example, in the 1980s, between Somalia and Ethiopia, Uganda and Tanzania, China and Vietnam, Iraq and Iran, Argentina and Britain), no other state, not even a close partner or ally, has become involved. The conflicts have been fought out in relative isolation.

But the great majority are civil wars. These one might expect to be the *most* local in character; yet, paradoxically, it is in those cases that outside states most frequently become involved.

Often the seriousness of such wars is hugely intensified by intervention of that kind. In a few cases external interference is mainly responsible for there being any war at all: as when a rebel force that would have had no significance but for outside assistance is built up to contest an existing government's rule (the Pakistan-created revolt in Kashmir in 1965, the US-orchestrated and financed rebellion in Nicaragua from 1981 onwards, or the South-African controlled rebellion in Mozambique today). In other cases the rebel cause could not be sustained for any length of time without external support.

Intervention in local wars can cover a wide spectrum of

activities, ranging from the despatch of arms of one kind or another, the provision of "advisers" (as by the United States in Vietnam in 1961–5 or by Cuba in Nicaragua and other countries), the supply of "volunteers" (as by China to Korea in 1950) or mercenaries (as in the civil wars in the Congo and Angola), the control of puppet forces (such as Israel's control of the South Lebanese Army, and Libya's control of a Moslem contingent in Chad) and the despatch of armed forces by an ally (for example, the Cuban forces sent to Angola and Ethiopia), to large-scale intervention by a super-power with its own forces (as by the United States in Vietnam and the Soviet Union in Afghanistan). Such activities may be open (as in the super-powers' involvement in Vietnam and Afghanistan) or clandestine (as by the CIA in a number of countries, and by British SAS and Iranian forces in Oman). Finally, intervention is sometimes undertaken in support of a government (as was the case for most of the actions undertaken by Western powers in the early post-war years) and sometimes on behalf of a rebel force (as with actions undertaken recently by the United States under the so-called Reagan doctrine).

The extent to which local wars are internationalised in this way has increased dramatically in the last 50 years or so. The decline of distance has meant that political events in a given state are now of far greater concern than before to the governments of neighbouring countries. These are no longer willing to avert their eyes from developments which they believe may be of considerable strategic importance to them. But, since they do not desire direct control — that is, sovereignty — in the contested area, the simplest way of safeguarding their interest is to help like-minded factions engaged in civil war, rather than mount direct trans-frontier attacks.

Intervention of this kind is characteristic of a world of ideological competition. It was already widespread in the inter-war period, when that competition began (as, for example, in the intervention in Russia by anti-Communist forces in 1917–21, in Hungary by Romania in 1919, in Spain by Germany and Italy in 1936–9). Since 1945, as ideological competition has become even more intensive, intervention too has increased. It occurred in Greece, on behalf of Communist forces, in 1946–9;

in Lebanon, on behalf of both Western and anti-Western forces, in 1958; in Indo-China, in support of either side by East and West, in 1961–73; and in the Congo, as assistance to different factions, in 1960–4. It has been undertaken especially by super-powers on behalf of the political forces they favour in areas of strategic concern to them: for example, by the Soviet Union in Hungary in 1956, in Czechoslovakia in 1968 and Afghanistan in 1979; and by the United States in the Dominican Republic in 1965, in Grenada in 1983 and in Lebanon in 1983–4, and (more indirectly) in Guatemala in 1954, in Cuba in 1961 and in Nicaragua and other places today. But such actions are also undertaken by lesser powers concerned about political developments in a neighbouring state: as by Egypt and Saudi Arabia in Yemen in 1963–7; by Syria and Israel in Lebanon from 1975 onwards; by Vietnam and Thailand in Cambodia from 1978 onwards; and by South Africa in Angola and Mozambique and other neighbouring states.

There are particular situations that make such intervention especially liable to take place. Where a sensitive area falls into a state of chaos and confusion as a result of civil conflict, a neighbouring power has more incentive to intervene (because such a political vacuum may invite intervention by a rival power), and more opportunity to do so effectively. So both Syria and Israel were encouraged to intervene in Lebanon as a result of the chaotic political situation after civil war broke out there in 1975; while in Afghanistan the turmoil created after the revolution of 1978 by the doctrinaire excesses of the Amin government, the conflict between two rival Communist factions, as well as revolts by a number of rebel groups, promoted intervention by the Soviet Union there. Especially where it appears that a victory for one side in a civil war may lead to the loss of an important strategic area to a political opponent, a neighbouring power may feel it necessary to intervene to maintain the *status quo*; so China in Korea, the Soviet Union in Hungary and Czechoslovakia, the United States in Cuba, the Dominican Republic and Nicaragua, were concerned to prevent, or reverse, the loss of neighbouring, strategically important areas to potentially hostile regimes.

Where such an intervention is believed necessary, there is no shortage of suitable justifications which can be found for it. Since governments cannot say that they have intervened to prevent a particular type of government from coming to power, they have to produce more acceptable explanations. Thus intervention can be said to be undertaken to restore law and order (as in the case of the Soviet interventions in East Europe and Afghanistan); to defend democracy (the US excuse for intervention in Nicaragua and Cuba); to counter an intervention, or possible intervention, by others (as with US involvement in Vietnam or that of North Vietnam in response); or even on humanitarian grounds, to protect a population from being oppressed by its own government (as when Vietnam intervened in Cambodia). Since such interventions are interventions in *civil* conflicts, by their very nature they are often not even considered by the United Nations, and the validity of such subjective justifications is rarely subjected to the impartial scrutiny and evaluation of an international authority. The legitimacy of intervention may thus go largely unchallenged. It is increasingly taken as a fact of contemporary international life that powerful states are likely to interfere in the domestic affairs of less powerful countries when they believe their vital interests are affected.

Whatever reasons are given for its action, the intervening power often finds it more difficult than it has anticipated to bring the operation to a successful conclusion. It finds that the local situation cannot be so easily brought under control as it had anticipated. As a result it finds itself increasingly heavily embroiled, often in embarrassing ways, in the complexities of local domestic politics. This political quagmire may prove even more sticky and intractable than the military quagmire. So the United States in Vietnam, the Soviet Union in Afghanistan, Egypt in Yemen, and Syria in Lebanon found themselves obliged continually to intervene (usually with little success) in the internal political system of the country they largely controlled. Local people, even their own protégés, have often proved stubbornly resistant to their patron's influence. The latter feels obliged continually to exert pressure to make its client government appear more attractive to the population of the country it rules: by modifying its policies or changing its personnel.

Sometimes the intervening power may find itself obliged to overthrow, and even to assassinate, the leaders it is supposed to be assisting (as when Diem was killed in a US-tolerated coup in 1963, and when successive Afghan leaders were deposed, and one murdered, after the Soviet invasion in 1979). These difficulties have limited the military, as much as the political, success of intervention (as we have seen in Chapter 1, the military and political are closely intertwined). Lesser powers have fared no better in this respect than greater ones. So Syria, despite its dominant military power in Lebanon, has never been able to control effectively the immensely complex political process within that country, any more than Egypt was able to control that of the Yemen, racked by continual political and sectarian conflict during the 1960s, or than India has been able to control the political system in the part of Kashmir it holds (being obliged continually to intervene to impose the leaders it favours or even to establish central government control there).

But there is another reason why intervention, even by powerful states, may fail. The very fact of intervention creates a new situation which can adversely affect the intervening power. The most obvious case is that intervention by one state leads to intervention by another to help the opposite side. So increased involvement by the United States in South Vietnam brought increased involvement by North Vietnam (and *vice versa*); increasing intervention by Syria in Lebanon brought increased intervention by Israel; growing external assistance given to rebels in Afghanistan (or Nicaragua) brought growing external assistance to the governments of those countries; and so on. The main object of the intervention may thus be nullified. In addition, the fact of intervention demonstrates the dependence of the force being assisted, whether govenment or rebels, on external support; and this may ultimately weaken rather than strengthen it. Finally, intervention may focus world attention on a situation which otherwise might have been largely ignored, and create demands for withdrawal and non-interference, which can be politically damaging not only to the intervening power but also to the force being assisted.

These negative effects of intervention result ultimately from one key fact: intervention is normally undertaken not in the interests of the state assisted but in those of the state that does the intervening. There are occasional exceptions. India's intervention in Bangladesh in 1971 was genuinely humanitarian in aim: to save the population of Bengal from the ravages of the invading Pakistani forces. When that purpose was accomplished, India rapidly withdrew its forces and did not attempt to exploit its dominant military position to secure political benefits. But in the majority of cases this has not been the situation. The Soviet Union intervened in Afghanistan to promote Soviet, not Afghan, interests; Syria intervened in Lebanon to promote Syrian, not Lebanese, interests; the United States intervened in Vietnam, and is intervening in Nicaragua today, for US, not Vietnamese or Nicaraguan, purposes. This discrepancy of aims usually becomes more apparent with time. It may eventually bring conflict even with those forces which are being assisted: for example, in Chad even the faction Libya claimed to be assisting finally turned against it. But these damaging effects of intervention often become apparent only too late, long after the original decision to intervene has been undertaken.

So in many cases intervention proves counter-productive. But the fact that intervention may be counter-productive does not prevent it from occurring. At the time the decision to intervene is reached, the *apparent* benefits which may be secured, and the possible dangers that may be overcome, are more visible than the embarrassment and complexities which may follow. It may at first appear relatively simple, by a judicious act of force, to sustain a friendly government in power against its opponents; or even to overthrow an unfriendly one. Little attempt is made, in most cases, to analyse carefully the political difficulties likely to be faced at a later stage; still less to look at the wider and more long-term consequences, for relations with other states, or for international society as a whole, and to balance these against the immediate short-term gains. It is scarcely surprising that it is nearly always the short-term considerations which appear decisive.

Reducing the destructiveness of local wars

The increasingly widespread practive of intervention means
that the localisation of war is to some extent an illusion.

Most wars today are localised only in a strictly geographical
sense, in that the fighting is confined to particular, relatively
restricted areas, usually a single country. But *participation* in
such wars often extends much more widely. In a very few cases
— as in the Korean and Vietnam wars, for example — the
forces of a number of states become involved, even though
their territory is never at any time touched, nor likely to be
touched, by the fighting. In other cases — as in Yemen, and
Afghanistan — one or two external states, usually immediate
neighbours, become heavily involved, despatching their own
powerful forces to help one side or the other. And often a
considerable number of states are more indirectly involved, in
supplying armaments and advisers, or at least offering political
support, to one side or the other. As a result of these activities
the same external powers become involved in a number of
wars. Such wars therefore, even if geographically limited, are
seen by many only as individual campaigns in a much wider
contest: a world-wide civil war, undertaken simultaneously on
a number of different battlefields throughout the world.

Such conflicts are internationalised in another sense. Dis-
tances, political and military, are much shorter than before.
Even local conflicts, therefore, become matters of deep concern to many other states, even distant states, in a way that was
rarely true in earlier days. A war in South-East Asia, however
much it may be geographically localised, may become the
principal focus of world attention over a decade, and its outcome may be thought to have a vitally important impact on the
world balance of power. A war in the Middle East is of critical
importance not merely to that region but to the world as a
whole. This is partly because there are now world-wide institutions whose task it is to deal with such conflicts. But it is, far
more, because their outcome can affect the interests of large
numbers of other states, including the super-powers and their
allies, all over the world. The shrinkage of distance has the
effect that there are no longer any purely local conflicts. All

have repercussions far beyond the area most directly affected. All can affect the strategic interests of many states. War, like peace, is today indivisible.

The conflicts of the present age, therefore, are local (or "regional", to use the contemporary jargon) only in appearance. Their repercussions are often world-wide. This is as true of many civil wars as it is of international wars. It is no longer possible, therefore, to say, as in 1945, that the international community, in seeking to maintain world peace, should close its eyes to domestic conflicts on the grounds that they are matters of direct concern only to the states where they occur and do not require the attention of the international community as a whole. In theory this is the principle on which the United Nations was founded. Its Charter provides that "nothing contained in the present Charter shall authorise the United Nations to intervene in matters which are essentially within the domestic jurisdiction of a state". It was largely on these grounds that the Vietnam War, though by far the most serious war of its decade, and though there was large-scale international intervention on both sides, was scarcely even discussed by UN bodies throughout the 15 years it continued. It is partly for the same reason that a substantial proportion of the 20 or so wars which are taking place today (see p. 169 below) have also not been discussed by that organisation.

But if civil wars today represent the great majority of the wars which occur, if they become a major focus of world attention, if there is frequently a substantial measure of external intervention in such wars, and if they therefore frequently represent as clear a threat to international peace and security as external wars, they need to be considered by international bodies as much as any other type of conflict. At present the United Nations' practice is totally inconsistent. Some civil wars — for example, those in Greece (1946–8), Lebanon (1958), the Congo (1960–4), Yemen (1963–7), Cyprus (1964), Lebanon (1975–), Afghanistan (1979–) and Cambodia (1980–) — have been considered; and in most of these cases action of one kind or another, including the despatch of peace-keeping forces or the appointment of mediators, has been taken to resolve them. But in many other cases — as in the civil wars in

Nigeria (1967–70), Ethiopia (1961–), Chad (1962–), the Philippines (1970–), Western Sahara (1975–), Uganda (1981–5)
and Sri Lanka (1983–) — no such action has been taken, even
where there is undoubted external intervention. It is not easy
to find any clear distinction between the civil wars which have
been discussed by the Security Council and those that have not.
External intervention was as manifest in the cases of Vietnam
and Chad as it was in Greece, Lebanon and Yemen; the civil
war in Nigeria in 1967–70 endangered the peace of West Africa
as much as did that in the Congo in 1960–4; that in Ethiopia
today, which has rarely been discussed, is as serious in its scale
and has caused far more casualties than that in Rhodesia,
which was endlessly debated.

We shall consider in greater detail below (Chapter 8) the
erratic practice of the United Nations in this respect, and the
way its procedures might be reformed to make it more effective
in dealing with local conflicts. But the United Nations is not the
only forum which has a role to play. Regional organisations
could be more active than they have been in the past in seeking
to resolve the conflicts within their own continent, and in
particular in seeking to prevent or deter external intervention.
The regular Western summits, at which the principal industrial
powers are represented, and which now in practice discuss a
wide range of current issues, not all economic, should more
regularly discuss major conflicts which threaten the peace of
the world, however local in origin (for example, those of
Central America and the Gulf region today). Finally, it is
obviously necessary that the "regional" conflicts should be
discussed in bilateral exchanges between the super-powers,
especially if one of them is directly concerned (see Chapter 5
below).

The obvious need, where such discussions take place, is to
try to *insulate* these conflicts, so deterring external intervention. It was at one time a recognised rule of international law
that there should be no intervention in civil conflicts of other
states (see p. 85–6 below). This rule, in so far as it was
observed, did often have the effect of localising such wars. The
implication was that the outcome of domestic conflicts should
be dependent only on the balance between *local* forces (on the

grounds, perhaps, that this should reflect the balance between the popular appeal of those forces). Thus no action should be taken by outsiders which might exacerbate or prolong the conflicts, or artificially distort their outcome.

If the dangers which arise today from intervention in local conflicts are to be reduced, there is clearly advantage in reviving that convention. There are obvious difficulties in doing this. In practice, while many states will vigorously denounce any intervention undertaken by their opponents (as the United States denounced Soviet intervention in Czechoslovakia and Afghanistan, and the Soviet Union has denounced US intervention in Nicaragua or Grenada) this does not in any way deter them from intervening themselves where the opportunity or need arises. Thus a rule of non-intervention is only likely to become widely accepted if it is applied consistently, and firmly demanded by third states, not themselves directly involved. Regional bodies, such as the Organisation of African Unity (OAU) and the Organisation of American States (OAS), could act more firmly than they now do in discouraging and denouncing intervention in the wars of their own region, regardless of ideology; and it is those organisations that are likely to have the greatest influence in discouraging intervention by the states within the region. But it is especially important that the United Nations should, more consistently than in the past, seek to establish and enforce the principle of non-intervention. The ruling of the International Court of Justice that support for the Contra operation against Nicaraguan territory from Honduras is contrary to international law demonstrates the current opinion of the large majority of the world's leading international lawyers on the question. The firmly established principle of non-intervention established within the inter-American system, many times reaffirmed, expresses the same principle. The Declaration on Friendly Relations among States, passed by the UN General Assembly in 1970, setting out a more detailed code governing intervention by one state in the domestic conflicts of another, reasserted the same rule. Those injunctions are unlikely to be influential unless they receive constant reaffirmation and redefinition.

More important than verbal admonitions of this kind would

be consistent *action* to demand non-intervention in particular cases: when such conflicts are considered by the United Nations, for example. One particular form this action can take is the *neutralisation* of a particular territory. When intervention takes place, it is often defensive rather than offensive in intention. It occurs above all where a neighbouring state, formerly friendly and like-minded in ideology, is taken over by a politically hostile regime (Nicaragua in 1979); or appears in danger of being so (Hungary in 1956); or is threatened by rebellion and disorder (Afghanistan in 1979). In such a situation a mutual agreement on neutralisation may offer the best way to reconcile conflicting interests: the smaller state is assured of the right to determine its own *political* future, without this representing a threat to the *military* security of the neighbouring super-power. An understanding which provides for neutralisation — forbidding an alliance with external powers or the presence of foreign forces, perhaps limiting the size of a state's armed forces and the level of military assistance which may be provided from outside — may thus be the best way of providing reassurance to other states in the region that political change represents no threat to them; and so of reducing the danger that they may intervene.

But ultimately the most important principle that the UN could seek to apply in such cases is that the ultimate settlement should provide for democratic elections, if necessary under international supervision. All civil wars represent a struggle for legitimacy. Each side, in seeking to establish its own legitimacy, claims to be more representative of the people as a whole than its antagonists are. A demand that the people themselves should be given the opportunity to decide between the rival claims, in elections held for that purpose, is thus one that is difficult for either side to reject. It provides the single element of consensus on which a settlement may be based. It is assent to that principle, therefore, which outside bodies and governments, seeking to end the fighting, should above all demand.

It is easier to state the principles which should govern the settlement of such conflicts than to apply them in individual cases. But the first step is to recognise that it is these so-called "local" disputes — the Vietnams and Afghanistans, wars in the

Middle East and the Gulf — which today represent the principal threat to world peace, not the confrontations along the
East–West border, where no realistic threat of war exists. If
world peace is to be preserved, therefore, it is to the dangers of
these local conflicts, not of the unbelievable East–West nuclear
exchange of popular imagination, that attention now most
needs to be directed.

4 The Failure of Interventionism

We have seen in preceding chapters that the typical way in which states make use of armed power in the modern world is not by all-out war against another state but by armed intervention, without declaration of war, in neighbouring states.

This is true not only of super-powers intervening in neighbouring territories to protect their own security. It is equally true of lesser states: so Yugoslavia, Bulgaria and Romania intervened in Greece in 1946–9; the United Arab Republic in Lebanon in 1958; the United Arab Republic and Saudi Arabia in Yemen in 1963–7; Pakistan in Kashmir in 1948–9 and 1965; Indonesia in Malaysia in 1963–6; Syria and Israel in Lebanon from 1975 onwards; Somalia in Ethiopia; Libya in Chad; China in Vietnam; South Africa in neighbouring states; and so on. Cuba, Libya, Syria and Iran have in a more general way sought to promote revolution within other states.

How successful have these various attempts at intervention been, and what has been the role of military power in securing success?

It cannot be said that the average level of success, whether for large powers or small, has been impressive. In a few cases where overwhelming power has been available and could rapidly be made decisive — as in Hungary, the Dominican Republic, Czechoslovakia and Grenada — *immediate* success has been achieved; though even in these cases the short-term gains have to be weighed against the long-term costs (for example, the stimulation of resentment in the region concerned against the intervening power and the creation of a more unstable international community generally). South Africa's raids against its neighbours may have brought temporary respite, the destruction of small cells of opposition; but only at the cost of intensifying the hostility of all neighbouring states, especially those whose sovereignty has been violated. There is reason to doubt the long-term gains from Israel's two invasions of Lebanon, which involved considerable loss in lives and international good name but won almost no measurable improvement in Israel's security. Syria's intervention in Lebanon may have brought it some prestige, but has given it no effective control of that unhappy state's labyrinthine political processes. Libya's long intervention in Chad brought temporary success for the faction it favoured but ended in utter defeat, both for that faction and for Libya itself.

But in the majority of cases intervention in civil wars has not even brought this degree of success. Normally there has been no immediate spectacular victory. More often assistance has begun, as in Vietnam, on a relatively small scale; and the commitment has gradually grown, until the external forces (often, as in that case, on both sides) are undertaking more of the fighting than the local ones. But, whatever the scale of the effort made, victory has proved elusive. It is not only the Americans in Vietnam and the Russians in Afghanistan who have found that even large-scale military endeavours win few rewards. Iraq seeking to exploit the apparent divisions among the Iranian people in 1980, Pakistan seeking to fan rebellion among the Moslem population of Kashmir in 1965, Egypt sending her crack troops to Yemen, Indonesia in tiny East Timor, South Africa in Angola, India in Sri Lanka, have all found it difficult in practice, even when possessed of overwhelmingly superior military power, to impose their will effectively.

The degree of success achieved has not differed greatly whether assistance is given to a government or to a rebel force. In either case the outcome has normally depended on factors other than the balance of military power. Aid to governments has succeeded somewhat more often, if only because governments already control the key levers of power. But if a government's control is weakening anyway, there is little evidence that external assistance can normally keep it in power. 500,000 US troops, with relatively sophisticated equipment and vast amounts of ammunition, could not keep Thieu in power in

South Vietnam: they could only maintain him a few years longer, at heavy cost in American lives and prestige. 50,000 Egyptian troops, modern aircraft and military advisers, could not bring long-term survival in Yemen for the government they were assisting. Substantial arms supplies from the United States could not bring victory for Chiang Kai-Shek over the Communists in China. The fact is that the effect of such military assistance, even on a considerable scale — even of massive intervention by foreign forces — is always relatively minor in relation to the local *political* factors which are ultimately decisive.

But, if aid to governments has often not succeeded, aid to rebels has proved even less successful. Assistance from three different countries could not procure victory for the Communist forces in Greece. Nasser's assistance to a variety of rebel movements in the Middle East failed to bring about the revolutions he had hoped to see (and even when revolutions occurred, as in Iraq and Syria, they produced no deep loyalty to Egypt). Saudi Arabian help to rebels in Yemen was little more successful than Egypt's to the government forces there. Somalia's support for an uprising among the Somalis in Ethiopia ultimately failed to win victory for their cause. The Bay of Pigs operation in Cuba won little local support and was over in two or three days. And the assistance being given by the United States to rebels in Nicaragua, Angola, Afghanistan and Cambodia today shows equally little sign of bringing about the downfall of the governments that are under attack there (pp. 92–103 below).

There are a number of reasons for this persistent failure of external intervention. The first and most obvious (as we saw in Chapter 1) is that, even in the most bitter civil conflict, whether or not a government holds or regains power is never primarily decided by military action. It depends on a wide range of factors, of which military success is only one. Far more significant to a government's survival are the policies it pursues towards its own population and the way that that population perceives them. If the leaders are manifestly corrupt, consistently unjust or incompetent, if social deprivation is widespread and inequalities insupportable, no government will easily retain power, whatever the balance of military forces may be and whatever degree of support it may receive from elsewhere. Even massive military assistance from an external power will always be relatively marginal in relation to factors of that kind.

It is for similar reasons that, in the absence of favourable political factors, aid to rebels is so often unsuccessful. The fact that they are enabled to harry the forces of the government, to blow up railway lines or ambush government troops successfully, even to capture a provincial city for a while, will not in itself be sufficient to bring them to power, unless they can also win the sympathy and support of large sections of the population. There is no difficulty in maintaining and equipping a force capable of undertaking destructive actions of that kind at considerable cost in lives and livelihood. But (as the examples of Nicaragua, Angola, Afghanistan and Cambodia at the present time show) there is no reason to suppose that this will be sufficient to overthrow the government in question. That government may suffer economic costs and social disruption — even "destabilisation". But this in itself is not enough, as current wishful thinking suggests, to bring about a change of regime. On the contrary, such actions may have the effect of uniting the people behind an otherwise unpopular government against what may appear as a foreign-inspired aggression. The ultimate factor determining all such conflicts, the attitudes and beliefs of the people concerned, cannot be moulded by military means. Whether the MPLA or the UNITA prevails in Angola, whether the Soviet forces or their opponents prevail in Afghanistan, depends not on what any external power may do, nor the power it can dispose of, but on the beliefs and loyalties of the local population, which will be little influenced by military factors.

There may even be an inverse relationship between military power and political influence. The larger the military force that is sent from the outside, the greater its visibility and the greater ultimately, in many cases, its unpopularity. Pumping ever more troops, ever more weapons, ever more advisers and support personnel into Vietnam did not make the United States more politically influential there; if anything, the reverse. In the eyes of many of the local people it merely signified the subservience of the country to an external power, the submergence of the local culture and way of life, the recruitment of more and more of the population to the provision of services, sometimes of an unsavoury kind, to the occupying army, and, above all, the total dependence of the local leaders on external support. All this is equally true of the Soviet Union in Afghanistan: its ability to hold down that country will depend not on the scale of its military support to the local regime, but on whether it can persuade the regime to establish the political and social conditions which will win it popular support. Whether the Duarte government survives in El Salvador will depend mainly not on the amount of *military* assistance provided by the United States, but on its *political* influence — for example, in preventing arbitrary killings, securing land reform and promoting economic progress. Whether the MPLA government succeeds in Angola depends not on the number of Cuban troops it can call on but on political, social and tribal factors influencing popular allegiances there.

In all such cases, therefore, it is hearts and minds which ultimately determine the issue. But hearts and minds are not necessarily influenced by military power. It is for this reason that the interventions which have been so widely undertaken in recent times have in most cases proved costly failures. They have, however, added considerably to the scale of each conflict and the total loss of life. And they have converted essentially local disputes into world-wide confrontations.

The legitimacy of intervention

The effect of intervention, however, has to be judged not only on the basis of its success in determining the outcome of particular civil conflicts. Even more important is its effect on the character of international relations generally: the nature of international society.

Few questions in international politics have been so bitterly disputed as the propriety of intervention in civil wars elsewhere.

Under traditional international law, governments were held to be under a "duty", once rebels had acquired control of a substantial part of a national territory, to recognise the "bellig-erency" of the insurgents. Once this recognition was granted, they were under an obligation to provide no assistance to either side. Recognition of that kind was usually highly unwelcome to a government fighting a rebellion. Not only did it deprive it of the possibility of receiving active assistance from elsewhere; it also accorded a recognised status to the rebel faction. For this reason the British government caused great offence to the US federal government by recognising the belligerency of both parties in the American civil war, and thereafter adopting a position of neutrality. A later British government caused equal offence to the Republican government in Spain in the 1930s by adopting a position of "non-intervention", meaning it pointedly refused to allow assistance to that government, at a time when Hitler and Mussolini were actively assisting Franco's rebel forces.

Since 1945 these old rules have been largely abandoned. No government now ever formally recognises the "belligerency" of a rebel force, so committing itself to strict neutrality. Instead a different, and simpler, rule has been widely recognised (though not always observed). Generally speaking, assistance to a recognised government has been regarded as legitimate; assistance to a rebel force seeking to unseat it has not. That was the principle used to justify the despatch of US forces to Lebanon in 1958 and again in 1983; of British forces to East African countries in 1964; and of French forces to assist a number of governments in Francophone African countries over the last 20 years. The same principle was proclaimed by the United States, and supported by many in Western Europe, during the Vietnam War: assistance by the United States to the established government, whether or not it could be called "democratic", was legitimate; assistance by North Vietnam to the rebel Viet Cong was not. Conversely, Communist govern-ments have been vigorously denounced when suspected of giving armed assistance to rebels in other countries against an established government.

The rule has been generally recognised irrespective of ideol-ogy, and irrespective of whether the government in power has been democratically elected. Of course, Western spokesmen have denounced especially vigorously assistance given by Communist governments to Communist rebels: for example, in China, Greece, Indo-China or (allegedly today) in El Salvador. But the same rule has been applied in other situations. Even when there has been substantial sympathy for a rebel cause (as in the case of the Ibo revolution in Nigeria, the struggle of the Kurds in Iraq, or that of the Eritreans in Ethiopia) it has none the less been generally accepted that in principle outside governments should not give them active assistance and support. The rule has even been applied when the regime against which the revolution is waged is manifestly undemocratic or even tyrannical. However much the right-wing dictatorships of Somoza, Trujillo and Batista, of Amin, Nguema and Marcos, were disliked, it was not thought proper to give active and overt assistance to revolutionary movements seeking to unseat them; and Western statesmen certainly would not have approved of direct assistance to those movements by other governments — for example, Communist governments. Perhaps the clearest indication of the fact that assistance to rebels is regarded as contrary to the accepted rules is the great care that has generally been taken to *conceal* such help when it has been given: thus the efforts of the CIA in helping to overthrow the government of Guatemala in 1954, of Iran in 1953, of Syria in 1956–7, of Indonesia in 1958, of South Vietnam in 1963, and of Chile in 1973, these and countless similar actions all had to be undertaken as covert operations, which would never be freely admitted by the government responsible.

Over the last few years this well-established convention appears to have been abandoned, at least in the US. Since 1980 the US government has provided open assistance to rebel forces in Nicaragua, Angola, Afghanistan and Cambodia. It has not sent its own armed forces to take part in these conflicts and is unlikely to do so (the only occasions when US forces have been used in war since Vietnam were the brief and successful intervention in Grenada in 1983 and the ill-fated expedition to Lebanon in the following year). But it is apparently no longer seen as reprehensible to provide help of other kinds, including the direct despatch of arms, to rebel forces in other states, and to be seen to be doing so.

This is a fundamental change in beliefs about what is permissible in the conduct of international relations: so fundamental that it is perhaps surprising that it has not aroused more comment around the world. It is a change which is far more visible in US policy than in that of other Western countries. In Europe it continues to be generally believed that assistance to rebels, even against authoritarian or non-representative governments, is contrary to the rules. No European government (indeed, no other Western government) has joined the United States in providing military assistance to rebels in any of the four countries mentioned. Even the British government, generally the West European government most supportive of the United States, has discreetly criticised US actions in Nicaragua.

No doubt in part this abstention merely reflects the fact that European states are no longer world powers, as the United States is. But it mainly reflects a difference of judgement. Europeans remain concerned about the effects on the stability of international relations generally should assistance to rebels become a normal practice throughout the world: about, that is, the question of principle involved.* But in addition they have grave doubts about the *prudence* of such a course in the particular cases where it has been adopted.

The point of principle can be stated fairly simply. It is generally accepted that, if stability is to be maintained in international relations, a few elementary rules are required. It was in the interests of stability that the traditional principles of sovereignty, and so the rule of non-intervention in civil wars elsewhere, were developed. It is, in this view, of little use proscribing "aggression", direct cross-border attacks by one state against another, if they are simply replaced by cross-border *assistance* to those engaged in violence in other states:

---

* It is notable that even Margaret Thatcher, the European leader most favourable to the Reagan administration, expressed this viewpoint in declaring, five days after the US invasion of Grenada, "If you are going to pronounce a new law that wherever Communism reigns against the will of the people . . . then the United States should enter, then we are going to have really terrible wars in this world." This is a viewpoint that would be shared by most European governments.

in other words, by a world-wide civil war, undertaken entirely within the borders of particular countries. The simplest way of avoiding this situation has been to stick to the rules outlined above: assistance to governments is permissible but assistance to rebels is not.

It is a rule which, it would seem, it is in the general interest, and in the interest of the West, to maintain. If it becomes generally accepted that large-scale assistance may legitimately be given to rebels in other countries, Western nations would be unable to complain when similar actions were undertaken by the Soviet Union, Cuba, Nicaragua, Libya, Iran and other countries supporting revolutions against governments which are seen as the West's friends. It would not be easy to contend that it was perfectly all right for the United States to assist the Contras in Nicaragua but disgraceful for Nicaragua to assist rebels in El Salvador; that the United States may assist rebels in Afghanistan, but the Soviet Union must not do so in Baluchistan; that the United States may help the UNITA forces in Angola, but Angola (or the Soviet Union) should not help rebel forces in Namibia or South Africa; that the United States may help rebels in Cambodia but the Soviet Union must not do so in the Philippines. If assistance to rebels came to be generally accepted as legitimate, it would become impossible to reject the right of Iran to assist rebellion in the Gulf states; of Syria to do so on the West Bank; of Cuba to do so in Haiti; of Ethiopia to do so in the southern Sudan; or of Libya to do so in Chad. In other words, it is not possible to consider the merits of the policy by taking individual cases in isolation. It is necessary to consider its impact on the conduct of international relations generally: on the character of contemporary international society.

There are two principal arguments used by supporters of the current policies. First, some claim that they too regret the breakdown of the traditional rules, but that it is not they who have brought this about but their opponents. US assistance to rebels is only *retaliation* for comparable help given by the Soviet Union, Cuba and others to rebels elsewhere. On this view, help for the Contras would not be necessary but for the help given by Nicaragua (or Cuba, or both) to rebels in El

Salvador; help for UNITA would not be necessary but for the help Angola is giving to SWAPO in Namibia; and so on.

This argument, however, is not convincing. First, it does not apply in many cases where the policy is practised. It is not suggested that the governments of Afghanistan and Cambodia are at present helping rebels in other states (though Afghanistan might be tempted to do so — for example, on Pakistan's north-west frontier, where there is a long tradition of rebellion among people of similar stock to the Afghans, or in Baluchistan, where there has been simmering unrest for decades; and it is possible that Vietnam might seek to do so in the troubled north-east of Thailand). The argument only marginally applies to Angola, since Angola merely provides refuge for SWAPO rather than actively assists it. And it is even questionable whether the argument applies to Nicaragua, since the amount of help which the government of that country can afford to rebels in El Salvador, with which it has no common border, is at the most extremely limited. More to the point, this is not the argument which the US administration itself has used. Help is given to the Contras to get Nicaragua to accept a "pluralist" regime; to Savimbi to induce Angola to get rid of the Cubans; to the coalition in Cambodia to get Vietnam to withdraw; to the rebels in Afghanistan to get the Soviet Union to withdraw: not as retaliation for help provided elsewhere. Indeed, if one looks at the world as a whole, it is no longer the case (as might perhaps have been said in the later 1940s and 1950s) that Communist states are busy everywhere providing assistance to rebels in other countries and seeking to undermine legitimate governments there (not even, it would seem, in the Philippines, though they must have been strongly tempted to do so). The tables have been turned: it is now the West, or rather the United States, rather than the Soviet Union, which is the main supporter of rebel factions: the "exporter of revolution".

The second argument sometimes used to justify assistance to rebels is that it is provided only against authoritarian regimes: in other words, to promote democracy. But this too is a difficult thesis to sustain. In the first place, it would be very difficult to amend the traditional rule in this way. In a civil-war situation it is not easy to define unchallengeably which are the forces that are "democratic" and which are those that are not.

Was Castro more or less democratic than Batista; the Sandinistas more or less democratic than Somoza; the Viet Cong more or less democratic than Diem; Franco than the Republicans; Mugabe than Muzorewa? Governments wishing to assist factions in another state will of course always claim that those are the more "democratic" forces. The Soviet Union has a different definition of "democratic" from that accepted by most Western countries, and would no doubt claim (even after the fall of Marcos) that in assisting the National People's Army in the Philippines — were it to do so — it was assisting the more "democratic" party. It does not seem, therefore, that even in general terms this is a distinction which it would be practicable or useful to apply. All it would do is to provide a ready-made justification for any intervention in any civil war elsewhere, and so hugely increase the degree of external involvement in the civil conflicts of other states.

But the argument is particularly difficult to sustain in the case of the assistance being provided to rebel groups in the four cases in question. There is unfortunately little in the records of the Contra leaders, or of the Pol Pot faction in Cambodia, to suggest that they are committed or credible exponents of democracy. And, though the governments against which their activities are directed may not be highly democratic either, they are no less so than the hundred or so other governments that have not been elected by the kind of democratic procedures approved in the West. If it is to be legitimate to provide support to rebels seeking to overthrow any government which is not fully democratic, the West would be engaged in assisting rebellions in most of the countries of the world. What distinguishes the four countries within which this assistance is at present given is not the fact that they are not democratic — a feature they have in common with countless others — but the fact that they have Communist, or at least left-wing, governments. And it is difficult to avoid the conclusion that it is this, rather than the nature of the constitutional system, which provides the main motivation for the assistance which is given.

There would seem, therefore, no adequate reason for the abandonment of the traditional rules concerning intervention. Those rules would appear to be very much in the interests of the West, and, indeed, of the world as a whole. Their violation appears to many as a dangerous development which could encourage the West's opponents to pursue similar policies in the very many civil wars which occur in the modern world. And it could, therefore, usher in a period of still greater instability in international relations than that which we have known since 1945.

Does the policy work?

But there is another reason for questioning current policies, and one that has nothing to do with general principles of this kind. It is simply that the strategy has not worked and, in the eyes of many, is unlikely ever to work.

To show why this is so it is necessary to look in some detail at the principal recent examples of the policy in operation. Before doing so it may be useful to set out the main reasons why the efficacy of the policy is questionable: reasons which apply, in different degrees, to each of these cases, and are likely to apply, wholly or partly, to most other cases where large-scale intervention in support of rebel forces is contemplated.

The first reason is that in almost every case the assistance is being provided to forces which have proved themselves militarily ineffective and, in the eyes of most observers, have no chance of achieving their objectives. The second, related reason is that these forces are also extremely weak politically, have little support in the country concerned, and in three of the four cases are fatally divided. The third reason is that the intensification of military conflict reduces, rather than enhances, the possibility of a political settlement, even though this is the apparent objective of the policy. The fourth reason is that the policy inevitably pushes the government against which the rebels are fighting further into the arms of the Soviet Union and its allies, so worsening the chances of accommodation between the government and the rebels, and so with the West, which it is in the West's interest to secure. The final reason is that it involves alliances with partners that are in most cases unattractive, unpopular and undemocratic: alliances which are therefore highly damaging to the long-term reputation and interests of those who are intervening.

All this can clearly be seen in the case of Nicaragua. First, the United States has been giving its assistance to an ill-assorted group of rebel factions which have few successes to their credit. Though frequently lumped together as "Contras", they have little in common with each other. There are three separate armies, under leaders who have been in constant conflict, sometimes highly publicised; and the most credible and "democratic" leader has now resigned. In the south the Contras have virtually ceased effective activity. In the north they have undertaken sporadic raids, often involving horrific violations of human rights, which can scarcely have endeared them to Nicaragua's population. Despite repeated attempts, they have failed to capture, even for a limited period, a single township which they could proclaim as a base or a rebel "capital". There is little evidence that they enjoy any degree of popular support in Nicaragua, which (as even the CIA would accept) is essential to any degree of military success. In other words, they have become a totally ineffective military force, which all the financial aid, training and armaments in the world are unlikely to make into a credible threat to the Nicaraguan government, with the substantial forces it has at its disposal. They have been able to provide repeated pinpricks, and a considerable economic cost, to the Nicaraguan government. But in general they have become a declining asset, which bring considerable political discredit to the US government in the region as a whole — ever resentful of US domination — for the sake of little political gain in Nicaragua itself.

Secondly, the Contras' military failures result from the fact that they have no political credibility. They represent no coherent political creed or force which can be held up to the people of Nicaragua as a reasonable alternative to the Sandinistas. On the contrary, the fact that they are, rightly or wrongly, still widely associated with the Somoza regime makes them highly unattractive to most Nicaraguans. And, because they can be portrayed as US puppets, dependent on US military and other assistance, it becomes easy for the Sandinista government to mobilise the population against them and so to win itself a greater degree of popular support than it would otherwise be able to enjoy. The unsavoury political reputation of their pro-

tégés damages the United States not only in Nicaragua itself
but throughout the region; while the recrudescence of US
interventionism, so long feared in Latin America, seems likely
to weaken US influence over the long term too. Nor is the aim
of bankrupting Nicaragua, which appears to have become a
primary objective, likely to be realisable, since the Soviet
Union, Cuba and other states, which have a strong national
interest in preserving the Sandinista regime, will, at whatever
cost, never allow the country to founder. The economic
deprivations such a policy brings about may temporarily erode
support for the government among some (though among
others it may equally well arouse a backs-to-the-wall determination to face the crisis). But there is not the slightest
prospect that the policy will bring about the downfall of the
regime. On the contrary it appears far more likely to harden
than soften its negotiating posture.

Thirdly, the assistance given makes it harder, not easier, to
arrive at the kind of political settlement which everybody
knows is finally required. In Central America that settlement
must be one under which Nicaragua pledges itself not to interfere in the affairs of other countries of the region, and possibly
even accepts some limitation on its procurement of arms from
elsewhere, in return for a resumption of normal relations with
neighbouring countries and the ending of US assistance to the
Contras. The longer the United States appears to be seeking to
secure its aims by force, and refuses even to negotiate with the
Nicaraguan government, the more it will lose the sympathy and
support of other countries in the region. The Contradora
states, and even the OAS, have increasingly insisted on the
need for a political, rather than a military, solution. And many
in Costa Rica and Honduras are becoming impatient with the
presence of the Contras on their territory. The other countries
of the region, as in the case of Cuba, will probably in the long
run come to terms with the prospect of a left-wing regime in
Central America (perhaps hoping eventually to be able to tame
it). The United States claims that its purpose is to bring about
negotiations between the Sandinistas and its opponents about
the establishment of a new political system. But, by intensifying the scale of conflict between the principal parties, it in fact

makes it less likely that such negotiations will ever take place.

Fourthly, in this as in other cases, the greater the military pressures which are brought to bear, the more the government under attack is made dependent on those who support it — in this case, forced to turn to Cuba and the Soviet Union for assistance. Just as Castro, who was almost certainly not a Communist when he came to power, was pushed into the arms of the Soviet Union by the isolation within Latin America which the United States deliberately imposed on him, so Nicaragua has been forced by similar pressures more and more into the arms of Cuba. The alternative of coming to terms with its neighbours, and perhaps in the long run being increasingly integrated into the Central American system, and possibly softened and civilised in the process, is excluded so long as Nicaragua is almost totally preoccupied with a battle for survival against externally supported rivals. The longer it remains dependent on Soviet support, the greater the degree of long-term influence the Soviet Union will be able to acquire within the region.

Finally, the interests of the United States, and so of the West as a whole, are seriously damaged by the nature of the company it keeps in Nicaragua. Some of the early Contra leaders, such as Cruz and Pastora, were no doubt genuine democrats, determined to see the establishment of a more liberal and democratic system of government in Nicaragua. But these are not the leaders with whom the Contras came to be mainly associated, either in Nicaragua or outside. Power increasingly gravitated towards the military chiefs — such as Calero — who had close associations with Somoza. In the eyes of the world, the Contras came to be a weird amalgam of mercenaries, Moonies and the CIA, but still primarily dominated by Somocistas. The demand from such people for a more democratic Nicaragua rings distinctly hollow. Whether or not a more democratic system can be established, in Nicaragua or elsewhere, by military measures must be a matter for doubt. But it certainly has become more and more unlikely that it could be brought about by those who have become the leaders of the Contra forces. The character of those leaders not only makes it difficult for them to win support within Nicaragua itself, but makes it dubious whether they represent a cause with which it is in the interests of the West as a whole to be associated.

In Cambodia many of the same considerations apply. Here too the groups being assisted have proved themselves ineffective as a military force. Their bases inside Cambodia were long ago destroyed by the Vietnamese and it seems unlikely that they will ever be allowed to regain a foothold. Though some of them — notably the Pol Pot forces — undertake occasional forays far into Cambodian territory, they are now based entirely on Thai soil. Given the universally acknowledged military prowess of the large Vietnamese forces, the idea that the rebels can win any long-term military success within Cambodia appears increasingly fanciful.

Secondly, in this case too, it is the political rather than the military weakness of the forces which has been particularly damaging. Even more than in the case of the Contras, they are hopelessly divided. Not only are there bitter conflicts between the three main forces of the "coalition" — there are well-attested reports of fighting between them — but there are also considerable divisions within each one of them. The Son Sann forces were for a time split altogether, a major faction repudiating Son Sann himself — the only figure, apart from Sihanouk, to enjoy any significant standing within Cambodia. The idea that a credible coalition could be established between the wily Sihanouk, the murderous Pol Pot — who was responsible for killing a substantial part of Sihanouk's family — and the former minister with whom he later quarrelled bitterly is one that no Cambodian takes seriously. Here too support is being given to a force which not only has little prospect of military success, but has still less chance of winning political support among the Cambodian people as a whole.

Thirdly, here more than anywhere, the aim of assisting the rebels has run totally counter to other important objectives (perhaps because the policy in this case appears to have been forced on the US administration by Congress, rather than *vice versa*). One of the few hopeful signs in the area over recent times has been the desire of the Vietnamese government to broaden its contacts, to establish better relations with the countries of ASEAN (the Association of South-East Asian

Nations), especially Indonesia and Malaysia, and above all to improve its relations with the United States. The US administration made some hesitant responses to these overtures, as have US business interests. Moves by Congress to increase support for the "coalition" rebels thus ran totally contrary to these initiatives and have perhaps ensured that they came to nothing. Above all, they inevitably made it less, and not more, likely that the Vietnamese would soon withdraw from Cambodia, which was said to be one of the main objectives of US policy.

Fourthly, here, most obviously of all, the effect of assistance to the rebels has been to push Vietnam still more firmly into the arms of the Soviet Union. Since China has shown itself even more hostile to Vietnam than the West, the only possible source of arms, finance and expertise for Vietnam is the Soviet Union. This relationship has already enabled the Russians to acquire valuable facilities at Cam Ranh Bay. An exclusive dependence on the Soviet Union is not in Vietnam's interests, and probably not its wish. Yet, the greater the military pressure brought to bear against Vietnam, the less freedom of action it will enjoy, and the less likely it is to seek a better relationship with the West, or to loosen its grip on Cambodia. The military threat from the guerrillas has not been sufficient, and will never be sufficient (any more than that in Nicaragua), to enforce the concessions demanded (such as elections, or a coalition government in Cambodia). Yet it has been enough to justify the Vietnamese in remaining in the country so long as it is continued.

Finally, here too it is impossible to reconcile support for the rebel coalition with the West's commitment to support democracy and respect for human rights. The coalition today is more than ever dominated by the Khmer Rouge, who are not only hard-line Communists, but are responsible for probably the most appalling violations of human rights since Hitler: the deliberate and premeditated slaughter of a vast number of their own citizens. It is difficult to think of any alliance which could be more damaging to the honour and reputation of the West. It can be explained only on the basis of a cynical disregard of the political principles which the West professes to stand for. Assistance for a group with such a record is totally incompatible with the West's professed respect for human rights (as well as with its justified denunciation of the very same people when they were in office). It can be defended only by those who believe that any action directed against an ally of the Soviet Union can always be justified, no matter what the means employed.

Assistance to rebels in Afghanistan has at first sight far more to be said for it. The invasion of that country by Soviet forces, and the resulting imposition of a Soviet-backed government, makes any opposition an honourable one. Any assistance given to that opposition therefore appears eminently justifiable. But in this case too there may be doubt how far such a policy can be productive over the long term. First, though the guerrillas have had remarkable isolated successes, and have even held strategic areas such as the Penshieh Valley over significant periods, their prospects of finally prevailing are questionable. Their operations are undertaken by relatively small-scale groups, under tribal chiefs, with no true co-ordination of their activities. They lack the equipment and the organisation to hold substantial areas, let alone inhabited towns, for any length of time, and they have shown themselves increasingly vulnerable to Soviet helicopter gunships. Like the rebel forces in Nicaragua and Cambodia they are deeply divided, on both religious and political lines. They have considerable nuisance value and can hold down considerable numbers of Soviet forces in Afghanistan, but have little prospect of long-term victory.

Secondly, their political effectiveness is also dubious. While undoubtedly patriots, concerned to rid their soil of Russian invaders, they lack any clear-cut political programme or political objective. While a few are committed to the establishment of a Western-style democracy, the majority are traditionalists, and often religious fanatics of a fundamentalist kind. They remain divided among seven highly factious groups. It may be doubted if, in the minds of ordinary Afghans living in Afghanistan, they present any clear image of a reforming movement which will offer a better way forward for the country. The fact that they are based in Pakistan certainly does not endear them to many Afghans, since there is a long history of enmity, and even sporadic fighting, between the two countries over the last 40 years. Nor, probably, are Iran and China, from which they also receive arms, better-loved patrons. They thus suffer from the same difficulty as similar groups elsewhere: they cannot survive without substantial assistance, but, the greater the assistance they receive, the less they appear as genuinely indigenous nationalist fighters. Meanwhile the huge refugee population in Pakistan is the cause of considerable resentment there, and creates strong political pressure on the Pakistani government to promote a settlement.

Thirdly, as in other cases, the more deeply the West becomes committed to the support of the rebels, the more difficult it may be to secure the kind of settlement, including a Soviet withdrawal, which most wish to see. As in Cambodia, the greater the military threat that is presented, the harder it is for the occupying country to withdraw. Western offers to recognise the neutrality of the country are unlikely to be sufficient to induce a withdrawal so long as the Russians continue to fear that when they go the guerrillas may win the upper hand (the failure of the Nkomati agreement on Mozambique shows how uncertain agreements of that kind can be). So far the efforts of the UN Secretary-General's special representative to promote negotiations for a settlement, even an indirect one, between the Afghan and Pakistani governments, have failed; and they may continue to do so as long as large numbers of rebel forces have a safe base in Pakistan. Once again, therefore, a reliance on military pressures may in practice inhibit the kind of political settlement which is, anyway, ultimately required.

Fourthly, as in other cases, the policy of assisting the rebels has only bound the existing Afghan authorities still closer to the Soviet Union. Admittedly their dependence is anyway so deep that it might not be appreciably diminished even if guerrilla activity were to cease altogether. But eventually an Afghan government which was less dependent on the Soviet Union for military support might become politically more flexible. Afghans are above all a proud and independent people and this tradition must to some extent affect even the existing government. It has made some attempt to conciliate the traditionalists in the population and to abandon, or at least postpone, its more radical reforms. If it were no longer in a position to plead military pressures as a reason for an authoritarian policy, that tendency would be increased. And the Russians would be deprived of the main justification for their presence in the country.

Finally, there is, in this case too, at least a question-mark about the political cause to which the West has committed itself. The Afghan guerrillas are something of a rag-bag. But the principal leaders (and some of those who have fought most effectively) are fundamentalist Moslems of an extreme kind. Some see the Ayatollah Khomeini rather than Western political leaders as their model: they are receiving military assistance from Iran as well as from China and the West. And it is by no means certain that the cause for which they are fighting resembles in any significant way (except in being anti-Russian) any that most in the West would identify with. Even to the people of Afghanistan they must often look like forces of the past rather than those of the future. And this is a further ground for questioning whether or not Western states have become too deeply committed to assisting their cause.

Many of the same arguments apply to Angola, the latest recruit to the band of countries with US-financed guerrilla forces. First, although it cannot be said that those forces have had no military success, it is less certain how far the successes they have had have resulted from their own efforts or from the substantial degree of South African assistance, in armaments, training and finance. Spectacular raids on diamond mines in the north, or the blowing-up of the Benguela railway, do not necessarily indicate any capacity to hold large areas of countryside, let alone substantial towns. UNITA's support has always been partly tribal (based on the Ovimbundo tribe) and may not extend much outside the south-east corner of the country. So, although the United States here is not backing a totally hopeless cause, as in the case of the Contras and the Cambodian guerillas, it is by no means sure that it is backing a winner.

Secondly, the same considerations affect the long-term political appeal that UNITA can expect to have. Savimbi, the movement's leader, is articulate, and skilled in winning sympathy for his cause in such countries as South Africa and the United States. But this provides no indication of the extent of his political appeal within Angola. The fact that he has been so dependent on South African support suggests that that appeal is limited. Even in the unlikely event of his defeating the combined forces of the MPLA and the Cubans and becoming the country's ruler, he might then only face years of revolution and civil war of the same kind as the present government has confronted. This would not matter so much if the objective was not victory but simply to harass the MPLA and to induce it to make concessions on the Cuban issue, or on Namibia. But in that case a new problem would arise (as over the Contras in Honduras): if those concessions are duly made and a settlement is arrived at, what happens to the guerrilla army now that it has achieved the only objectives the United States had in mind for it?

Thirdly, just as much as in all the other cases, the support for guerrilla action is difficult to reconcile with the long-term political objectives the West claims to stand for. Here, as in most of the other cases, it is freely recognised that it is a political solution rather than a military one which is ultimately sought. That is why the US representative Chester Crocker became involved in long and complex negotiations, juggling with a range of variables which includes the presence of the Cubans, Angolan support for SWAPO, South African support for UNITA, sporadic South African raids against Angolan territory, and a settlement in Namibia. The delicate equations required to resolve all these difficulties simultaneously have not necessarily been made any easier to balance with the additional complication of direct US support for Savimbi. The result may have been to make the Angolans feel more dependent on Cuban forces, and more reluctant to see them go, at least until a very late stage in the settlement process. In such a situation a crude desire to screw up the pressure may, far from forcing a concession and so ultimately bringing a solution, only make a solution more difficult to secure.

Fourthly, here too the military pressures created may have only made Angola more dependent than ever on the help of Cuba and the Soviet Union. The latter countries, feeling that the United States is seeking to achieve its aims in Angola by a policy of increasing confrontation, are led to conclude that they have no choice but to meet that challenge. Cuban forces, far from being withdrawn, are more likely to be increased. Support for SWAPO, instead of being reduced, could be intensified. Far from exercising restraint over the internal problems of South Africa (as they have so far), all three countries might seek to exploit them to their own advantage. The end result of increased assistance for Savimbi might therefore be not only greater instability in Angola, but greater instability in Southern Africa as a whole, with all its dangerous consequences.

Finally, US support for UNITA may be, in a still more damaging way, detrimental to wider political objectives in Southern Africa as a whole. For, in an area of predominantly black African states, it places the West in the position of seeking to weaken the government of one such state; and puts it in close alliance with South Africa in seeking to bring that about. There is today an increasingly close understanding between the black states of the region, based partly on their common hostility to South Africa, but also on the closer economic ties now being established between them (partly with Western assistance). For the United States to make itself the declared enemy of the Angolan government, and to seek to overturn it by force, thus damages the future Western position not only in Angola itself, but throughout the region. Above all, by placing the West in alliance with South Africa it puts in question its declarations of hostility to the apartheid system in that country, in a way that could be damaging to Western interests throughout the whole of Africa and even beyond. Nor is such a policy easy to reconcile with the West's ultimate objectives in South Africa itself. There the long-term goal is to bring about a peaceful transition to majority rule without endangering the stability of the region as a whole. To join South Africa in support for Savimbi will *reduce* the West's ability to bring pressure for change in South Africa, while *increasing* the instability of the surrounding region. It will certainly make less likely the kind of agreement between South Africa and Angola which must lie at the heart of a long-term settlement in Namibia. At the same time the policy provides the perfect opportunity for the Russians to score easy propaganda points. It is hard to believe that this is a course which can be in the long-term interests of Western countries, still less of the international community generally.*

These recent cases of intervention are of course only the latest in a series of operations of the same kind carried out since 1945. Most of these equally failed to secure their objectives. Between 1949 and 1953, for example, the CIA trained and equipped a considerable force of several hundred Albanian émigrés, who were sent out on a number of expeditions against Albanian territory in the hope of winning local support and instigating a successful revolution there: in fact the agents secured virtually no local support, caused no embarrassment to the Albanian government, and the only consequence was the death or imprisonment of hundreds of men. In Syria in 1956–7 the CIA twice tried to organise coups to overturn the government there; both attempts failed, because the necessary political conditions did not exist. In 1957–8 the Agency organised a substantial rebellion in Indonesia against the Sukarno government, trained and equipped the forces involved, and flew them in CIA planes (one CIA pilot was, embarrassingly, captured by the Indonesians), but the rebellion secured little support and was a military failure. In Laos from the end of the fifties until 1973 the CIA conducted a "secret war", in which it organised

---

* A similar point has been made by John Stockwell, who was in charge of the CIA's operations in Angola in 1974–5, when the Agency was helping both Savimbi and Roberto Holden against the MPLA. He points out that, despite the CIA's having committed $31 million to opposing the MPLA victory, the latter had "nevertheless decisively won" and "15,000 Cuban troops were entrenched in Angola with the full sympathy of much of the third world". The only result was that the United States was "solidly discredited, having been exposed for covert military intervention in Angola's affairs, having allied itself with South Africa and having lost" — *In Search of Enemies* (New York, 1978), p. 272. According to Stockwell, "many other officers in the CIA and State department thought the intervention irresponsible and ill-conceived, both in terms of the advancement of US interests and the moral question of contributing substantially to the escalation of an already bloody civil war, where there was no possibility that we would make a full commitment and ensure the victory of our allies".

an army, which was at one point 40,000 strong, including 15,000 from Thailand and thousands from other countries of the region, while US planes undertook sustained bombing raids from Thai air bases: raids which, according to a Senate report, were designed "to destroy the physical and social infrastructure of Pathet Lao-held areas" and "helped to create untold agony for hundreds of thousands of villagers".* And a whole series of operations against Cuba from 1959 to the early 1980s, of which the Bay of Pigs operation was only the most spectacular, failed because the local population did not rise in support in the way that had been anticipated. All these operations failed for the same reason as those we have described: because, even though it was possible to mobilise a substantial degree of military power, that power could not prevail where the political conditions were not favourable. Military power alone, however overwhelming, was not the decisive factor.

Conclusions

In none of these cases, therefore — those of the eighties no more than those of earlier decades — has interventionism proved successful.

If there is one single fallacy which encapsulates the errors of that policy it is this: in every case it is assumed that it is possible

---

* Albania 1949–53: for a full account, see Nicholas Bethell, *The Great Betrayal* (London 1984).

Syria 1976–7: these events are described in W. Eveland, *Ropes of Sand: America's Failure in the Middle East* (New York, 1980). Eveland was a member of the National Security Council on loan to the CIA at the time in question.

Indonesia 1957–8: for details, see J. Burkholder Smith, *Portrait of a Cold Warrior* (New York, 1976).

Laos: quotations are from the staff report prepared for the US Senate Sub-committee on Refugees, Committee on the Judiciary, 28 September 1970. See also F. Branfman, *Voices from the Plain of Jars: Life under an Air War* (New York, 1972), p. 5: "Village after village was levelled, countless people blown up by high explosive, or burnt alive by napalm and white phosphorus, or riddled by anti-personnel bomb pellets." Branfman was a community worker in Laos in 1967–71.

to solve what is essentially a political problem by military means. If sufficient military pressure can be brought to bear, it seems to be believed, opponents can be *compelled* to concede what they would not otherwise be willing to accept: a change in the political system, a coalition government, the withdrawal of Cuban, Soviet or Vietnamese forces.

But this calculation rests on a basic misconception. It is possible that if, in the cases considered above, the United States had been willing to intervene directly and with the maximum force at its disposal, it would have succeeded in imposing the solutions it desired, at least for the short term (though it may be doubted how long such imposed settlements would endure, and what the military cost of seeking to maintain them might be). Yet, as the case of Vietnam shows, even with large-scale intervention success is not guaranteed. The relatively small-scale guerrilla forces that the United States has recently assisted can do far less. They are capable of causing considerable difficulties, repeated aggravations, a series of pinpricks, to the governments concerned, but (even with US assistance) nothing more. The military pressures available are thus, in every case, not strong enough to compel the concessions required on matters of vital interest to the governments concerned; yet they may be just enough to prevent the *political* accommodation which provides the only alternative hope of an understanding. If the rebels were more powerful there would be no need of an accommodation: they would simply overcome their opponents and impose their own type of regime (though whether that would in every case be preferable is a question of judgement). But, given that they do not have that power, all that assistance to them normally achieves is to harden the position of the government under attack and make it a matter of honour for it not to negotiate under military duress. The failure of the policy in these cases represents, therefore, a vivid illustration of the thesis presented here: that military means are usually ineffective in securing political objectives. More important, in the long term the policy involves the deliberate injection of instability into the international environment. And it sets an example which, if widely followed, could be gravely embarrassing to the West as a whole. Traditionally, and over many years, it has been considered that the West has an interest in stability rather than the reverse. There would seem to be no reason to believe that that interest has changed today.

It is not only, therefore, on grounds of principle that it is undesirable that the traditional rule concerning intervention in civil wars elsewhere should not be overturned. It is equally because all the evidence suggests that the policy of providing assistance to rebels is unlikely to procure the objectives that have been proclaimed for it.

5 The Super-power Relationship

In preceding chapters we have argued that there is today less and less danger of an armed confrontation between East and West in Europe: least of all one in which nuclear weapons are employed. On the contrary, warfare in the modern world, we have seen, is increasingly localised, taking place mainly in the form of civil conflict in developing countries. Such conflicts, however, are aggravated by competitive intervention from outside, often by the super-powers. This suggests that one of the most important ways by which the dangers of war in the modern world may be reduced is by the development of understandings between those powers about how intervention may be reduced, and local conflicts resolved, through political accommodations.

Traditionally, when representatives of the two super-powers have come together over the past 30 or 40 years, it has been assumed that the main topic for discussion between them must be questions of disarmament, or at best major bilateral issues in dispute at the time in question. But it is increasingly recognised today that a major theme for discussion at such meetings — perhaps even the principal subject of negotiation — should be the numerous "regional" conflicts occurring in various party of the world, in many of which those super-powers are themselves involved, directly or indirectly. Discussions about these regional conflicts may, many believe, be more relevant to the real problems of the modern world than the endless negotiations about nuclear weapons and other forms of disarmament that have proceeded so interminably over the past 40 years, with so little apparent outcome. They will, after all, relate to the kind of wars that actually take place today rather than to the dangers of an all-out East–West confrontation, which few now think likely. The regional conflicts themselves usually involve one or other of the super-powers, occasionally both, and appear a more likely cause of a direct confrontation between them, even if only with "conventional" arms, than the situation on the East–West frontier. Indeed, since it is these conflicts that are usually the main source of tension between them at any one time, an accommodation over them may be the essential condition of reaching an understanding on the more fundamental relationships between East and West. Far from being an irrelevant and unimportant sideshow, therefore, these conflicts, and the disagreements between East and West about the way they should be resolved, lie at the very heart of the matter.

So what are the chances of institutionalising these discussions? What kind of arrangements and understandings, even direct trade-offs (such as Soviet concessions in Afghanistan matched, say, by US concessions in Nicaragua) might be reached to reduce their dangers? Above all, are there any general principles governing super-power conduct in such areas that might provide the basis for a wider consensus over disputes of this kind, and so reduce dangers in the future?

Many of the most bitter East–West conflicts of recent times show only too clearly the lack of such a consensus at present. Conflicts have occurred in many different parts of the world in which the super-powers were not originally directly concerned but into which they have been increasingly drawn, usually on opposite sides. Often each supports rival factions in a civil war (as in Vietnam, Afghanistan, Nicaragua and Angola, for example). The actions taken by one of them to support one side, whether government or opposition, is seen by the other as unacceptable interference in the affairs of another state, or unjustifiable support for an unrepresentative regime. There are no agreed principles governing the limits of intervention by outside powers in such conflicts that might provide the basis for accommodation or for restraint on super-power action.

What is more, because each side judges each situation in subjective terms, often hugely magnifying the evil intentions and Machiavellian activities of its opponent, there is little

willingness to apply objective standards. Each power, it sometimes seems, wishes to apply one set of principles in one sphere
and a different set in another. Thus the Russians appear to
believe that their security interests justify them in seeking to
dictate what type of government comes to power in Afghanistan, but dispute the right of the United States to do the same in
Nicaragua or Cuba. Conversely, the United States may declare
itself justified in supporting revolutionary forces seeking to
overthrow the regimes in Nicaragua, Angola, Cambodia and
Afghanistan, claiming that they are undemocratic and unrepresentative, yet strongly resists efforts by other states to support
revolutionary forces seeking to overthrow established governments in other places (such as El Salvador, Chad, Lebanon or
the Philippines), efforts that are often based on similar claims.
Usually neither super-power is ready to concede that its own
conduct in one area is in any way comparable to that of its
opponent in another.

It seemed at one time that it might be possible to establish a
tacit understanding based on the principle of spheres of influence. The United States would generally allow the Soviet
Union a free hand in its border regions, such as Eastern
Europe; while the Soviet Union would allow the United States
the same in Central America and the Caribbean. For the first
30 years after 1945 this principle was generally applied: the
United States did not respond, except verbally, to Soviet interventions in Hungary and Czechoslovakia, nor the Soviet
Union to US action in Guatemala or the Dominican Republic.
Today that situation is changing. The Soviet Union has felt
obliged to provide arms — even if limited in capability so far —
to its new allies in Nicaragua, while the United States feels
equally justified in providing support for revolutionaries operating close to the Soviet border in Afghanistan.

Disagreements on the principles to be applied are thus more
intense than ever. To the Soviet Union, the West, in supporting rebels in Afghanistan, is deliberately threatening its vital
security interests in an area adjacent to its own border. But, to
the West, it is merely giving assistance to those who are justifi-
ably resisting a foreign occupation of their country.

In El Salvador the situation is reversed. Here it is the United

States which claims that the Soviet Union is supporting, at least indirectly through surrogates in the region, a revolutionary force seeking to overthrow a friendly government in an area close to the United States' own borders. Against this the Soviet Union and its allies claim that the rebel forces in that country are merely seeking to establish a more genuinely representative government in a country that has long been effectively controlled by a small and unrepresentative elite (and in any case deny they are giving any assistance to the revolutionaries).

In Cambodia, the United States and China are, in the eyes of the Soviet Union, cynically assisting discredited rebel factions that have even less right to call themselves democratic than the government of that country, merely in order to promote their own political and strategic ends. The United States and China, on the other hand, claim that Cambodia is an occupied country, and that they are merely helping the Cambodian people to throw off unwelcome Vietnamese rule.

Conversely, in the Middle East it is the United States which claims that the Soviet Union is giving support to disruptive regimes in Syria and Libya, more in order to do damage to the interests of the West than in pursuit of any discernible political principle or overriding national interest. The Soviet Union, on the other hand, would claim that it is merely responding to the requests of these countries for justified assistance, and making it possible for them in turn to help the Palestinians to defend their inalienable rights.

It is thus not easy to see any consistent principle being pursued by either East or West in its approach to these various regional conflicts. It can no more be said that the West only supports "democratic" forces than it can be said that the Soviet Union only supports "socialist" ones. The West in many cases supports authoritarian governments — for example in South Korea, Chile, Pakistan and Morocco — that are resisting demands for democratic reforms, while the Soviet Union gives its assistance to many governments that are by no means socialist. Nor can it be said that one side supports legitimate and recognised governments and other revolutionaries: both sides support both in different circumstances and all that can be said is that each supports those it believes to be its friends, whether they are in government or in rebellion against governments. Finally, it cannot be said of either that it intervenes only in its own immediate region, to promote its own immediate security interests; the Soviet Union has become increasingly involved, at least indirectly, in Angola, Ethiopia and South Yemen, just as the United States has been closely involved, whether directly or indirectly, in such places as Lebanon, Grenada and Afghanistan.

The search for principles

At present, therefore, there is little consensus between the super-powers on the principles that should be applied in negotiations on regional conflicts, and little consistency in the approach that each has taken in addressing the various conflict situations in which it has become involved.

Is it likely to be possible, therefore, to construct a set of more consistent principles that might govern intervention in civil conflicts elsewhere — that might, in other words, provide the basis for a more lasting understanding between East and West on such matters?

There is nothing new in the attempt to establish such principles. There have been many efforts at different periods to define rules governing the intervention of outside powers in civil wars elsewhere. One was the rule of traditional international law that, when a civil war had broken out and a significant part of a state's territory was occupied by revolutionaries, other states should recognise the "belligerency" of these forces (see p. 85 above). Once that had been done, those states were under an obligation to adopt a position of strict neutrality. This meant that no assistance should be given even to the legal government, let alone the rebel forces, since aid to either would constitute a violation of neutrality.

But, as we saw earlier, there is little evidence that governments took much notice of these alleged rules. In general, governments were inclined to adopt whatever policy they thought would best promote the national interests of their own states. In practice help was freely given to governments and revolutionary forces alike. After the Napoleonic wars, France helped government forces in Spain (1823) and rebel forces in Greece (1826–9); Russia helped government forces in Austria (1849) and rebel forces in Bulgaria and Bosnia (1876–8); Britain helped rebel forces in Portugal (1833–6) and government forces in Spain (1835–40); Prussia helped rebel forces in Schleswig–Holstein (1848–50) and government forces in Poland (1863). Even after the First World War there was not much more agreement on such questions. The major powers began, as in more recent times, to help the ideological factions with which they sympathised. So in the 1930s Germany and Italy assisted the rebel forces in Spain, while the Soviet Union helped the republican government there.

By the end of the Second World War, the old idea that governments should remain neutral in the civil wars of other states had been largely abandoned. Then, as we saw, there emerged a new kind of consensus. The general understanding came to be that intervention was legitimate when it was in support of an accepted government, but not so on behalf of revolutionaries. This view certainly was strongly supported in the West. Western politicians consistently denounced as "subversion" assistance to rebels elsewhere, regardless of whether a government was "democratic" or otherwise. Communist governments were widely condemned when it was believed they were giving support to rebel movements: for example in China, Greece, Vietnam and other parts of South-East Asia, in Bolivia, Uruguay, the Dominican Republic and other parts of Latin America, in the Congo, Angola and Rhodesia in Africa. There was a general presumption that the government in power possessed some kind of prescriptive right and, however unjust its policies, was to be brought down only by constitutional means. It was recognised that, if external support for revolution became the norm, a situation could come about in which rival external powers were providing assistance to revolutionary forces in almost every third-world state, sometimes in competition with each other. A policy of providing support to revolutionary movements elsewhere was therefore seen as a threat to international order almost as unacceptable as acts of aggression against the frontiers of other states. This was the type of argument employed by Dulles, when US Secretary of State, in denouncing the help China had allegedly given revolutionaries in South Vietnam, and by Selwyn Lloyd, when British Foreign Secretary, in denouncing Nasser's assistance to opposition forces in the Middle East as "indirect aggression".

This way of thinking now seems to have been abandoned, at least in the United States. There, as we have seen, it is no longer seen as wrong to provide assistance to rebel movements elsewhere, or necessary (when it is done) to conceal such action. In Nicaragua, Afghanistan, Cambodia and Angola, for example, direct and unconcealed action is undertaken to assist revolutionary movements on the grounds that these represent "democratic" forces seeking to overturn a non-democratic government.

Thinking in Europe has not yet adjusted to this radical change of belief and strategy. On that continent there remains substantial doubt about the propriety (and often about the prudence) of external assistance to rebel forces in any country, whatever the character of the regime. In particular, there is some perplexity concerning the principles that have been applied by the United States in deciding where such assistance is appropriate and justified.

If it is held that aid to rebels is justifiable in any case where a non-democratic government is in power, there would clearly be no shortage of suitable candidates. Something like three quarters of the countries of the world today probably have governments that cannot be said to be democratic under most normal definitions. To hold that it was justifiable to support revolution in any of these countries would create a highly unstable international society. But it would at least be a principle of a sort.

It is difficult, however, to recognise this as the principle underlying current policies. There are many governments all over the world that are by no means democratic but that none the less are seen as friends of the West. In such places — Pakistan, Morocco, Chile, the Philippines until recently — Western governments, and the US government in particular, do not view revolutionary movements with sympathy, however undemocratic the local governments are known to be. There would certainly be no willingness to accept that foreign assistance to revolutions in those countries, such as that given by the

United States in Nicaragua and Cambodia, was justified in those cases.

Conversely, in cases where revolutionaries in other countries *are* helped (as in Nicaragua and Cambodia) it is not always clear whether the object is to ensure for them the government the countries want or the government the United States wants. Is it really believed that the people of Nicaragua can want the supporters of Somoza returned to power, or that the people of Cambodia want supporters of Pol Pot? Can assistance to such forces really be presented as support for "democracy"? It occasionally seems that the principle of democratic choice applied by the present US administration resembles the principle of consumer choice once favoured by Henry Ford: have any government you like so long as it is not Communist (or even rather left-wing).

Nor is it easy to see that assistance is provided for revolutions at present where governments are *most* undemocratic: can it really be said that the governments in Nicaragua and Cambodia, which have had elections of a kind, however questionable, are those that are least democratic in the world (compared, for example, with those in Chile, Paraguay, Pakistan, or even China and Yugoslavia)? It would seem rather that the distinction is that the governments in the latter category, however undemocratic, are seen as friends of the West, while those in the former category are seen as its enemies. It is this distinction, rather than the niceties of the consititutional system in each case, that appears to determine whether or not a revolution should be helped.

If, therefore, any kind of consensus is to be arrived at with the Russians concerning intervention in regional conflicts, it is likely to have to be based on somewhat more objective principles than underlie current policy. There are obvious difficulties: domestic political constraints, ideological antagonism, believed strategic interests. But if the dangers such conflicts represent — to the super-powers themselves as much as to their partners — are to be reduced, understandings of a sort may be necessary.

What should be the basis of such principles?

Let us begin by considering the most fundamental aspect of

the problem: the strategic interests of the super-powers themselves. For the foreseeable future it seems likely that the super-powers will remain intensely interested in the type of governments that come to power, and the policies which those governments pursue, in areas of special concern to themselves. This applies particularly to areas immediately adjoining their frontiers. The record of their actions since 1945 demonstrates only too clearly the determination of the super-powers that political developments in such areas should not represent an unacceptable threat to their strategic interests. The Soviet Union directly intervened, through large-scale invasions by its forces, in Hungary in 1956, in Czechoslovakia in 1968, in Afghanistan in 1979; and undertook a show of force against Poland in 1981. By these means it has ensured that, except in the case of Yugoslavia in 1949 (a country that was in any case at the furthest extremity of its sphere of influence), no government ideologically unacceptable to it has been able to establish itself in Eastern Europe. The invasion of Afghanistan had a similar objective in another strategically vital area.

In much the same way, if less brutally, the United States too has intervened, directly or indirectly, in Central America and the Caribbean, to try to prevent left-wing governments coming to power in that region. Six such administrations have been formed throughout the Western hemisphere since 1945: in Guatemala in 1951, in Cuba in 1959, in the Dominican Republic in 1965, in Chile in 1971, in Nicaragua in 1979–80 and in Grenada in 1979. In each case the United States has intervened in one way or another to secure its overthrow, and failed to achieve that aim only in the case of Cuba in 1961 and in Nicaragua (so far).

Other countries have shown a similar propensity. Thus China has intervened several times in border areas: in Korea in 1950–3, on the Indian border in 1962 and in Vietnam in 1979 (in addition to reconquering Tibet and attempting to reconquer the offshore islands). South Africa and Israel have likewise intervened by force several times in areas close to their borders to protect their security interests. Such actions as these indeed represent the principal *external* use made of armed force in the modern world.

Is it therefore the case that, at least in immediately neighbouring areas, super-powers are certain to demand a veto over
the coming to power of politically unacceptable governments?
Must this therefore represent one element in any understanding to be reached between West and West concerning conflicts
in those areas?

To answer that question it is necessary to be clear about the
fundamental motives of each super-power in intervening in
that way. Though the *immediate* aim has always been to overturn a government, it is not the case that this was the *fundamental* concern. Of course the Soviet Union would prefer,
for purely political reasons, to see Communist governments in
power in Eastern Europe. But that has not been the reason for
its successive interventions. The reason has been to ensure that
a government does not come to power there that might, in
Soviet eyes, represent, directly or indirectly, an unacceptable
threat to Soviet security. Of course the United States would
prefer to see democratic governments in power in Central
America and the Caribbean. But that is not the fundamental
reason for its successive interventions (otherwise the United
States would have intervened in innumerable other cases as
well). The United States has intervened to prevent a government coming to power that it believes might represent, directly
or indirectly, an unacceptable threat to US security.

The demand among major powers for security in immediately neighbouring areas does therefore seem to be a fundamental feature of the contemporary international landscape,
and it is one that must be taken into account in any attempt to
arrive at settlements of the conflicts that arise within those
areas. It is not the case, however, as the record of these
attempts might suggest, that those security interests can only
be safeguarded by according those powers a total veto over
political developments in neighbouring states. That view has
come to be adopted, in practice if not in theory, because of a
failure to distinguish between political and strategic concerns.

In an ideological world fears become focused on political
doctrines, and on political factions that espouse those doctrines, rather than, as would be more logical, on the policies
that the factions may pursue. Super-powers have therefore

taken the view that their security interests can be safeguarded only if they are in a position to control the type of government that comes to power in particular areas. Thus the Soviet Union invaded Hungary — though the Western powers were totally uninvolved in the political developments taking place there, and though the new prime minister demanded nothing better than neutrality for his country — because it feared the emergence of a non-Communist government that might lead to uncontrollable changes throughout Eastern Europe, and so to an unacceptable threat to its security. The United States supported an invasion of Cuba in 1961, despite a very limited Soviet presence there at that time, because it was feared that the continued existence of a Communist-inclined government there might lead to unacceptable changes in Latin America as a whole. In all the subsequent uses of force — or support for its use — by both powers (the Dominican Republic in 1965, Czechoslovakia in 1968, Afghanistan in 1979, Nicaragua from 1981 onwards), the reasons have been similar.

There has been little disposition on the part of the super-powers to consider whether it might be possible to secure alternative safeguards for security that did not require the overthrow of the government concerned: whether, for example, the new regime might be willing to provide undertakings, concerning military dispositions and alliance policies, even concerning its political activities, that might provide the reassurance required. Above all there have been no efforts by the *opposing* super-power, whether through public statements or private undertakings, to make military action unnecessary by providing assurances that it had no intention of seeking political or military advantages from the new situation.

In other words, in all these cases the political and military consequences of a change of government have been regarded as inextricably joined. So long as this assumption has been maintained, the strategic interests of the neighbouring super-power could be seen to make the overthrow of the politically unwelcome regime an inescapable necessity.

If understandings are to be possible between the super-powers about such areas in the future, it is likely to be only through the delinking of these two elements: the political and the strategic. It is this that might make it possible for the peoples of small countries in the neighbourhood of a super-power to determine their own political future free of external interference, without representing any threat to the security interests of a neighbouring power. If there is any chance of finding solutions to the conflicts of this kind existing at the present time — in Nicaragua as in Afghanistan, in Cambodia as in El Salvador, in Angola as in southern Lebanon — it is likely to be along these lines.

A balancing of interests

How might this principle be implemented in practice?

The most obvious way would be by seeking a solution based on *neutralisation* of the area concerned. This is a formula with a long and respectable pedigree. It was applied to Switzerland after the Napoleonic wars; and that country has since been involved in no foreign war. It was applied to Belgium under the treaty of neutralisation of 1839 and to Luxembourg in the treaty governing that country of 1867; though these saved neither country in 1914, they did have the effect of bringing major powers to their defence which might not otherwise have assisted them. In more recent times the principle has been applied to Austria — a country lying precisely on the border between the two spheres of influence — since 1954; it was attempted unsuccessfully for Laos in 1962; and it has been adopted unilaterally by Finland and Sweden. The record is thus a patchy one. But it is certainly not so poor as to make the attempt to apply it once more in comparable situations a hope-less one.

One obvious case where it might be applied is in Afghani-stan. Afghanistan was in practice a neutral country until the revolution of 1978: a neutrality effectively recognised by both super-powers, each of which contributed to the development of the country before that year and neither of which sought to acquire a dominant position. It is unlikely that the Soviet Union will withdraw its forces, or allow an independent gov-ernment to emerge in Afghanistan, unless it receives assur-ances of the country's neutrality in the future. Recognition of that neutrality would need to be given not only by Western powers but also by China (whose influence in the area appears far more dangerous than that of the West in Soviet eyes) and Pakistan. Such a recognition could and should be matched by undertakings from the Soviet Union and Afghanistan that they would not intervene in the affairs of Pakistan (the northern borders of which are populated by Pathan people, more closely akin to the Afghans than to other Pakistanis and under strong Afghan influence), and particularly in the highly sensitive and unstable province of Baluchistan.

A formula based on neutralisation might also have a role to play in other areas. If the main concern of the United States in Nicargua is the potential threat the government there may represent to US security, and to stability in Central America generally, an essential element in any settlement may be undertakings by that government concerning its military and political alignments. These might include pledges concerning the number of military advisers from Cuba and the Soviet Union, and perhaps concerning levels and types of armaments. Even this might not meet US apprehensions unless it were accompanied by commitments concerning interference, military or political, in neighbouring countries, above all El Salvador. But pledges of this kind would not of course be given unless they were matched by undertakings of a comparable kind by the United States and Honduras that they will prevent intervention in Nicaragua launched from Honduran soil. And here too undertakings by the countries in the region would need to be matched by comparable pledges by external powers, such as Cuba and the Soviet Union. It is precisely because no region today is totally insulated from super-power rivalries that the projected discussions between the super-powers about regional conflicts can be of such importance.

In Cambodia, too, a similar principle may be applicable. It has always been apparent that Vietnam would be unlikely to withdraw its forces except in return for a cessation of all aid, whether from China or the West, to the coalition rebels. These matching undertakings would ideally be linked with a commitment to UN-supervised elections. A long-term solution will almost certainly have to include commitments against *future*

intervention, whether by Vietnamese forces or those of rebel
factions ensconced on Thai soil. Whether or not this is linked
to a formal recognition of neutrality (of the kind that Prince
Norodom Sihanouk so long demanded), some form of neutralisation of Cambodia is likely to come about (whose people
doubtless wish for nothing more than to pursue their own lives
free from foreign intervention). Though it is not likely that any
comparable neutralisation will be possible for Vietnam or even
Laos, the removal of the external pressures would at least
mean that Vietnam will no longer be pushed into the arms of
the Russians, as it has been by recent Western policies; and in
practice there are many signs, including the recent improvement in Vietnam's relations with the United States, which
suggest that Hanoi might welcome the opportunity to pursue a
more even-handed policy.

In all these cases, therefore, the principle of neutralisation
— in fact if not in name — seems likely to form a part of the
final settlement. For the super-powers themselves this represents in effect a kind of mutual self-denying ordinance. Usually
in such cases the concern of each super-power is not to win
unchallengeable political control for itself but to deny it to the
other. A settlement based on recognition that neither side will
be militarily dominant in these contentious areas is the obvious
way of procuring a settlement which may be acceptable to
both. Since it insulates the areas from East–West rivalries, it is
often a solution that is also welcome to the state most directly
concerned. Indeed, one of the benefits of such arrangements is
that they may provide a greater freedom of manoeuvre —
except in the military field — to the individual third-world
country in question. Many third-world countries wish for
nothing better than to be "non-aligned" and they are therefore
unlikely to feel too uncomfortably constrained in the one area
where they are limited. They will in consequence be freer to
choose the type of government that they wish for themselves,
rather than having to fear intervention whenever their policy
preferences stray too far from those of the nearest super-
power.

The principle that any settlement of a local conflict should
satisfy the strategic requirements of the super-powers is clearly

one that can be applied only in areas relatively close to their own borders. Of course, given the continual erosion of distance, especially strategic distance, in the modern world, it could be argued that each today has a strategic interest in almost every part of the world. And this means that some areas may be seen as important to the interests of both. The Middle East is essential to the interests of the United States because of its dependence on Middle East oil, as well as because of US links with Israel. But the Middle East is important also to the Soviet Union because it almost adjoins the USSR's own borders (much of it is far closer to the Soviet border than Grenada is to the United States). The Horn of Africa, though not of similar vital importance, is seen as of significant interest to both, because both have strategic interests in the area and both have client states that look to them for support.

Even so, most would accept that somewhat different principles apply to these more distant areas. Distant powers have less right to demand that their interests should be protected, and usually less capacity to ensure that they are, in these cases. Moreover, the interest is more indirect. The immediate interest may be that of some local state which is itself an ally of one or other of the super-powers. So, for example, both Israel and Syria have a direct interest in the settlement reached in Lebanon, just as both Vietnam and Thailand have an interest in the settlement reached in Cambodia; and each of these is supported by a super-power that will seek to ensure that those interests are protected in a settlement.

The more important difference, however, is not that the interest of the super-powers is more remote: as the size of the world declines there may be less and less willingness to acknowledge that there is any area in which they are not interested. The real difference is that both have an *equal* interest: something that cannot be argued in the case of their own border regions. In these cases therefore it is likely that rather different principles will be required in securing the settlement of regional conflicts, and that these will need to take account of the different geographical configurations.

It will mean that often *both* super-powers will need to have a voice in discussion of the settlement to be arrived at. For some areas this is not a principle that will be readily accepted by some in the West.

In discussions of the Middle East, for example, it has for many years been taken for granted that a major aim was precisely to *exclude* Soviet influence. Yet it is arguable that the West itself has an interest in recognising a Soviet interest. This results today not merely from the Soviet Union's geographical propinquity but from the position it has acquired as a supplier of arms and other assistance to many governments, as well as from its naval presence in the Mediterranean. So long as the Soviet Union feels that its interests are ignored and that it is being frozen out, it has every incentive to use its influence with its clients, above all Syria, in a way that is unhelpful to Western interests, and in a way that makes a settlement less possible. If brought into the process, it is more likely to use its influence to promote the prospects of peace in the area. The Soviet Union's interest in maintaining a fruitful super-power relationship, in avoiding being dragged into a dangerous conflict and in improving (as it now seeks to do) its relations with the less radical governments of the area (including Saudi Arabia and Israel) means that discussions are probably more likely to prove fruitful if it participates than if the Arab states negotiate in isolation.

It is now increasingly unlikely that it will be possible to negotiate a separate Israel–Jordan settlement on the lines of the Camp David accords, as many had hoped and as Israel would still like to see. The recent rapprochement betwen Jordan and Syria, Yasir Arafat's refusal to accept UN Resolution 242, as well as the reluctance of the Likud members of Israel's coalition to make the kind of concessions in the West Bank that would induce Jordan to take the plunge without the Palestine Liberation Organisation, make it likely that sooner or later Syria (and possibly Lebanon too) will have to be brought into the discussions. In this case the creation of the suggested "international forum", in which the Soviet Union (on whom Syria is so dependent) has a role to play, may enhance rather than diminish the chances of a settlement. Conversely, any proposed settlement that is not underwritten by the Soviet Union, and so by Syria, may have little chance of lasting success.

In the Horn of Africa a similar situation exists. Ethiopia, for all its economic and political difficulties, remains the dominant power of the region. There are even some signs that it might welcome a reduction in its dependence on the Soviet Union. But it is the presence of Cuban troops in that country that represents the factor of primary concern to many in the West. Here too, it is self-defeating to deny the reality of Soviet interests in the region: for it is concessions from the Soviet Union and her allies — above all the withdrawal of Cuban forces — that the West mainly wishes to bring about. In this case too, therefore, it may be necessary to recognise the right of the Soviet Union to a voice. As in the Middle East, each of the super-powers may have an important part to play in securing the co-operation of its own client states; and each may need to have a continuing role within the area, economic as much as political, if stability there is ever to be restored.

The presence of Cuban forces in Angola is another subject the US administration has hoped to confront in talks on regional conflicts. Here too it is unlikely that the Soviet Union will be willing to confine discussion of the question to that specific point alone. Indeed it has long been evident that the withdrawal of Cuban forces is only one element in a series of trade-offs that need to be negotiated if a settlement covering both Angola and Namibia is to be reached. Such a withdrawal is likely to be undertaken only in return for the cessation of all assistance, whether from the West or South Africa, to Savimbi's rebel forces. Similarly, an undertaking by Angola to prevent incursions into Namibia from its territory may need to be matched by corresponding guarantees of Angolan territorial integrity from South Africa. If it is the case, as Western spokesmen have often maintained, that the Cuban forces are merely "surrogates" for the Soviet Union, and that Cuba acts in this respect only on behalf of the Soviet Union, it may be logical (even if it is unwelcome to South Africa) that the Soviet government be directly involved in discussions. If Cuban forces are unlikely to be withdrawn without Moscow's assent, or if Angola is unlikely to accept their withdrawal without some external pressure, there is a good case for the Soviet government to become more immediately engaged than it is at present.

These three areas — the Middle East, the Horn of Africa, and Angola — are merely examples of current crisis spots that do not immediately adjoin either super-power yet in which each has some interest; they therefore could well feature in super-power negotiations. Other areas of mutual concern will no doubt continually be added to the list. South-East Asia generally, the Koreas, Chad, Western Sahara and the Antarctic are examples of other questions on which a degree of understanding between the super-powers would be valuable. Since the interests of each power are now world-wide, the potential agenda can scarcely cover less than the world as a whole.

The framework of negotiations

Is it possible to sketch out any general principles that might be observed in discussion of this kind?

The individual situations encountered in different parts of the world are of course unique, and it would be absurd to suggest that they can all be resolved according to some uniform formula to be applied in a mechanical way. It is none the less possible to suggest a few broad principles that could usefully be observed by those on both sides who take part in negotiations of this kind.

First, the simplest and most obvious is that it is important in all such discussions to understand what are the basic, and minimal, objectives and interests of the opponent. In most negotiations each side has objectives that may play a large part in their rhetoric, yet are not really fundamental concerns; while there are others — sometimes strategic considerations — that are rarely spoken aloud yet are often the most profoundly important. It is indeed precisely the purpose of negotiations of this kind to increase understanding of the fundamental interests and objectives of the opponent. It is only this which can reveal what kind of compromises may best reconcile the interests of each, and indeed of all parties (including the local governments and peoples). The objective must always be to secure a balance of advantage that, while it does not secure the maximum objective of either side, is none the less an outcome each can live with. This is precisely what the nineteenth-century Concert of Europe, operating through protracted and secret diplomatic negotiations, was often able to achieve: to resolve a number of local conflicts through settlements acceptable to all five major powers of the continent.

Second, it is important to seek settlements that will avoid provocation, especially military provocation, whether to super-powers or lesser states. As we have seen, there is ample evidence that the most powerful motive of the super-powers in recent times has been the protection of their strategic interests, and this aim has usually proved even more powerful than purely ideological objectives. No settlement that is incompatible with the strategic interests of either side, therefore, is likely to be possible (or prove stable if attained).

Third, there will be more chance of success if each individual crisis is discussed on its own merits and, so far as possible, divorced from extraneous considerations. There are sometimes apparent attractions in "linkage": in using concessions made in one area to extract corresponding concessions from opponents in another. But in most cases each individual problem — say, the Middle East — is already so complex that it is made virtually insoluble, or even more insoluble than before, if an attempt is made to inject cross-bargaining of this kind. It is almost certainly better, therefore, that discussion should be undertaken in separate compartments, probably by different teams of officials.

Fourth, the kinds of arrangements arrived at must not simply be imposed by the two super-powers to conform with their own interests, but must clearly take account of the interests and views of local governments and peoples. If this is not the case, a settlement is unlikely anyway to be enduring, and externally imposed settlements would then in time only discredit the entire system of super-power dialogue. What this means is that each of the super-powers needs at all times to remain in the closest contact with the local governments and groups concerned — above all their own partners and protégés — so that the super-powers may be understanding of the latter parties' concerns and in a position to secure the maximum possible consent for any arrangement arrived at. In the final resort local agreements can only be reached by local governments. The role of the super-powers, therefore, is rather to propose the general character such agreements may take and use their influence to secure their acceptance. In many cases it will not be easy to reconcile the views of local parties — if that were not the case there would be no crisis. And one of the benefits that the participation of outside powers may bring is that it may be easier for them to recognise the kind of compromise solutions that are necessary, and eventually to induce their local partners to show a similar realism.

For many conflict situations the only final answer is one that Western states should have no difficulty in supporting: a resort to democratic elections. Most of these conflicts result from situations of civil conflict — as in Afghanistan, Nicaragua, Cambodia, El Salvador, Angola and Western Sahara at the present time — where two or more factions are struggling for power, each invariably claiming to be "more representative of the people" than its opponents. The only unchallengeable way to resolve such disputes is by resorting to the polls: by allowing ballots, not bullets, to determine the issue. Admittedly it is still necessary to ensure that such elections are fairly and impartially conducted, if only to make it less likely that their results will subsequently be challenged: a condition by no means easy to fulfil, as many recent examples testify (for instance, the elections in Uganda in 1980, El Salvador in 1984 and in the Philippines in 1986 were supervised by international observers, but in each case the results were widely challenged). If Western governments are to be true to the principles they claim to stand for, however, the demand for fair, impartially conducted, externally supervised elections should play a central part in the negotiations undertaken on such questions.

Even if there were agreement on all these points — and not all of them are agreed at present — the negotiations could face problems. Though the proposal for regional discussions has so far been fairly widely welcomed, in Europe as elsewhere, it could come up against difficulties which need to be confronted. The idea of super-power discussion is welcomed mainly because it is disagreement between the super-powers about such matters that at present arouses most concern. That disagreement is not only dangerous to the super-power relationship, but may reduce the prospect of successfully resolving the conflict in question. The discussions between them, it is therefore hoped, may help reduce difficulties.

In time, however, a dialogue that was confined to the two super-powers might begin to appear increasingly exclusive. There could be pressure for the discussions to be opened up. When Far Eastern affairs are in question, it would not be unreasonable for China to wish to have its say, and even to denounce discussions about its own region in which it played no part. When questions concerning the Mediterranean, or even the Middle East, are discussed, Western Europe might increasingly wish to have a voice (especially since its view on those questions has in recent times often been different from that of the United States). When African trouble-spots are discussed, African states may begin to query the relevance of a discussion between two non-African powers, unless they themselves are in some way represented in those negotiations. And so on.

It may come to be believed that there is a need for something not altogether unlike the old Concert of Europe, but enlarged to cover the world as a whole: in other words a body far smaller than the Security Council, less cluttered with the representatives of several very small states, yet far more representative of the principal centres of power in the world than discussions confined to two states alone can be. Such a body would have to include, as a minimum, China, Japan and the European Community (in practice this would be a single Western European country representing the Community for a term). Even this would leave Latin America, Africa and South Asia unrepresented. In time these too might demand to be represented by suitable states (perhaps their own "great powers", Brazil, Mexico, Nigeria, Egypt, India), thus creating a body of nine or ten, not altogether unlike the five or six "great powers" that took part, with substantial success, in the negotiations of the Concert of Europe.

Such a prospect is of course still far away at present, if indeed it is ever realisable. Moreover, it could be argued that even if such a concert were finally to come about, it would be no substitute for continued regular consultations between the two greatest powers about the issues causing dispute between them. The latter talks are required only partly as a means of arriving at solutions to the difficult disputes that exist in many parts of the world, though it is certainly to be hoped that they may contribute to bringing about such solutions. They are required mainly as a means of reducing tensions and disagreements between those powers themselves, disagreements that may intensify local conflicts but are in themselves a source of danger.

For the next decade at least, such discussions clearly have a major part to play. It is thus important that the way in which they are conducted, the mechanics that surround the meetings, the spirit in which they are held, and the principles that they seek to apply are such as will maximise their likelihood of success. The allies of each super-power may increasingly seek a voice on such questions. This will reflect a recognition of the importance that the negotiations could have, if conducted in a genuine spirit of goodwill as well as realism, in helping to establish a more stable and peaceful international environment.

6 The Role of Western Europe

There is, therefore, a legitimate doubt whether the discussion of the world's principal trouble-spots should be left exclusively to the two super-powers alone. There are other centres of power, sometimes directly interested, that may have a useful role to play. This applies as much as anywhere to Western Europe. The combined gross national product of the countries of the European Community is larger than that of the United States or the Soviet Union. The Community's total population is greater than that of either. Its armed forces include the weaponry of two nuclear powers and over 2 million men under arms. Its members have long and rich experience of world politics. They are closely associated within an integrated political community which is a pioneer in international co-operation. They represent one of the world's richest and oldest cultures. Why then is their combined voice in international affairs so weak?

On all the great issues of today — above all those of disarmament — it is the United States and the Soviet Union which negotiate together to determine outcomes which affect many others. In some cases it may be claimed that the United States is representing Western Europe as well as itself. But this is a somewhat theoretical notion, since all US administrations are inevitably concerned primarily with US interests. Indeed, the most striking and deplorable feature of Europe's weakness today is the fact that its views carry so little weight with its principal ally in its conduct of an individualistic, high-profile and often combative foreign policy. In the actions it takes on most of the great issues of the day — the Middle East, Libya, Afghanistan, Central America, Angola, to name only a few —

the United States pursues its own policies almost entirely without regard for European opinion, and usually without serious consultation. To a substantial extent, in modern world affairs, Europe stands on the sidelines: an observer, but not in any real sense a participant.

The rhetoric of international diplomacy has spoken for many years of a "partnership" between the United States and Europe. President Kennedy spoke of the "twin pillars" of North America and Western Europe. Henry Kissinger inaugurated a "year of Europe" and devoted a large amount of time and effort to consulting European allies (even if individually rather than collectively), however frustrating he found the process and however little notice he took of the views he heard. Since then, year after year, with monotonous insistence, political leaders, foreign ministers, parliamentarians, commentators and the general public call for more "consultation" and better "co-operation". But, despite occasional desperate efforts to improve things, no real change takes place. Each part of the alliance continues to go its own way, with little regard for the views of the other.

But the consequences of this process are quite different for each partner. The difference lies in the fact that the United States, with or without European support, plays a dominant role on the world stage; while on most of the issues of international politics today the views of Europe go largely unheard.

Over the last few years understanding between the United States and Western Europe on foreign policy questions has perhaps never been worse. During that time glaring differences have appeared between the two on a succession of issues, including some of the most crucial questions of international politics: reaction to the Soviet invasion of Afghanistan, the boycott of the 1980 Olympic Games, European involvement in the construction of the Russian pipeline from Siberia to Western Europe, strategic exports to the Communist bloc, the Middle East, Southern Africa, policy towards Libya and towards terrorism generally, policy in the Persian Gulf, and a number of questions concerning disarmament and arms control — to mention only a few of the more obvious cases. In most cases the principle adopted by the United States has been to act first and consult later.

A typical case occurred in the bombing of Libyan targets by American planes in 1986. The terrorist acts complained of had taken place almost exclusively in Europe. The bombing itself was to be undertaken relatively close to Europe and from European bases. And any retaliation for the bombing was likely to take place predominantly in that region. Yet there was no attempt by the United States to consult Europe about the decision to bomb. Consultation took place only over the granting of over-flying rights by European countries, *after* that decision had already been taken (to be followed by complaints when some European states did not co-operate). Even on a question in which European interests were so directly involved, there was no attempt at meaningful consultation. Nothing could show up more clearly the deficiencies of the consultation process as it exists today, or highlight so well the sharp differences in attitude between the United States and most countries of the European Community on a major international question.

It is true that there has not always been complete agreement *within* Europe on some of these questions (as, for example, over Libya). But generally speaking, on the majority of world issues there has been a recognisable consensus among European members, with only the British government an occasional exception. And that consensus has been a measurable — and increasing — distance away from the policies pursued by the United States. Even over the Libya bombing, the intra-European differences were far less signficiant than those between Europe as a whole and the United States: the viewpoint of the British public was similar to that elsewhere in the continent; and it is doubtful whether any British government, even one led by Mrs Thatcher, would another time accede so readily to US wishes in flagrant disregard of the views of its European partners.

These differences did not begin with the Reagan administration. Even under President Carter and before, divergences of view were often visible. There has rarely been a time when commentators were not deploring the "state of the alliance".

The divergences have reflected differences in geographical perspective, with European foreign policy attention coming to focus increasingly on the European continent, while America's vision is that of a world power engaged in a global confrontation. They have reflected differences in ideological zeal, with the Europeans less inclined than US counterparts to see the Soviet Union as intent on world domination and its hand at work in every revolutionary movement around the world. But above all they have reflected a difference of temperament, between the more emotional and volatile US attitude — veering from near-isolationism in the immediate post-Vietnam era to ultra-interventionism since the 1979 Tehran hostage crisis — and the cautious pragmatism of the Europeans.

Though there have always been differences, the divergence of view became far more pronounced after President Reagan came to power. The hard-line anti-Communism and simplistic nationalism of US policies since 1980 have removed US actions and attitudes still further from those of Europe. For this reason it can no longer be said, as perhaps once it could, that it does not matter that the United States does not consult, because Europe anyway largely agrees with US policies. Europe no longer agrees.

The main reason for concern is not that these differences exist, though it is disturbing that they have become as great as they are. It is that so little attempt is made to reconcile them. The Europeans today no longer expect that their views will carry much weight with the US administration. And for that reason they make little serious effort to influence US policy — for example, on Central America, the Middle East or Afghanistan. Conversely, the United States no longer cares much what Europe thinks: it is increasingly concerned to determine its own policy on these and other questions on the basis of its own view of US and Western interests, not on that of the alliance as a whole.

The result is that, in practice, the policies of the West, and the actions by which the West is judged, are the policies and actions of the United States. Europe is to a large extent an observer and a non-participant. European states may occasionally ask their ambassadors to represent their views in

Washington on some aspect of US policy. Very occasionally they all do so together. But for the most part these efforts are ineffectual. The United States rarely takes much notice. The result is that, for all its wealth, power, population and experience, Western Europe is not today a significant actor on the world scene.

The world's political process is surely the poorer as a result. The long experience which European states have of world affairs, their continuing association and good relations with many countries with which they were historically associated, and their acknowledged political and diplomatic skills should give them the opportunity to play a far more significant part in international politics than they have recently undertaken. And the central position which Europe occupies, not only geographically but also politically, might enable it sometimes to play a valuable and much-needed role in the international political process: in particular, it could perform a useful function in improving relationships between North and South and between East and West — especially desirable in the current troubled state of those relationships — and so reduce the double polarisation of the world political system which may otherwise come about. This is a contribution to the creation of a more stable world community which we should not underestimate.

Areas for possible influence

What are the individual issues on which the lack of an effective European voice is especially damaging? A classic case concerns the Middle East. In the first 10 or 15 years after 1945, European states, especially Britain and France, were the dominant external powers in the Middle East. Though that situation could not have persisted (even without the folly of the 1956 Suez intervention), West European states, including Italy and Spain, did acquire during their years of activity in the region a rich fund of knowledge, experience and close working relationships. It is not unrealistic to think that they may still have something to contribute to the solution of the problems of the regime.

Instead, they have elected to accord to the United States sole responsibility for managing the peace process within the region. Such initiatives as the Kissinger shuttle, Camp David and more recent moves directed primarily at Israel's relations with Jordan have been conducted by the United States alone, with virtually no input from Europe. At one point, with great daring, the Europeans managed to interject the Venice communiqué, formulating a marginally new approach to the Palestine problem. They have undertaken a prolonged, if unpublicised "Euro-Arab dialogue". But it would be fatuous to pretend that these have had any significant influence on the affairs of the region. Sometimes, indeed, they appear to be intended as distant signals, designed to protect European interests in relations with their principal oil suppliers, rather than direct initiatives intended to bring about significant movement towards a settlement.

It is on the face of it by no means self-evident that the United States is the only outside power that can play a useful role in producing a settlement. Its close identification with Israel may make it better able to exercise influence in that country (though Israel's continued intractability, for example on West Bank settlements and policy in Lebanon, leaves some doubt about how effective even that influence is). But it may correspondingly reduce America's capacity to influence the Arab states, especially the more radical such as Syria, or the Palestinians, both crucially important factors in the next stage of the process.

It is now increasingly recognised that it may be necessary to offer a place to the Soviet Union, if only as Syria's main protector, in the "international forum" which some now expect to have a part to play. But it is arguable that Western Europe has an equal right to participate. Western Europe's interest in the region — geographical, historical, commercial and political — is at least as great as that of either of the super-powers. The Arab states have consistently encouraged Europe to take a higher profile in the discussions (admittedly, mainly because they believe that Europe will giver greater weight to their case). It is to be hoped that the discussions do not become polarised between the camps of Israel and the United States and the Arab states and the Soviet Union — a danger which mounting tension between American and Libya may intensify. If that happens, Europe could have a useful role to play as an honest broker. But it is unlikely to be able to do so unless it takes its courage in both hands and moves forward from the back seat which it has so obligingly occupied over recent years.

Southern Africa is another region where European countries — above all Britain and Portugal — have historically had far greater experience than the United States. Yet here too, as in the Middle East, they have recently been willing to allow the negotiating process to be monopolised by the United States. Until the Reagan administration came to power, the principal European states did play a substantial part in the search for a settlement in Namibia (and therefore in Angola). Britain, France and West Germany were all members of the so-called "contact group" which was accorded a recognised role by the United Nations in negotiating South Africa's withdrawal from Namibia and the settlement to be implemented in that country. Since 1980 that group has virtually withdrawn, leaving the field clear for Chester Crocker, President Reagan's special envoy. This move was perhaps based on the belief that the Reagan administration's "constructive engagement" policy might elicit a more co-operative response from South Africa than the Five had been able to do. In fact, by supporting South Africa's demands for the withdrawal of Cuban forces from Angola as a precondition for a Namibia settlement (and, in some observers' view, actively promoting that demand), American efforts may have made the chances of a settlement worse, not better, than before. And the new US policy of providing armed assistance (including Stinger missiles) to Jonas Savimbi's rebel forces will make its acceptance as an impartial mediator in the dispute still more unlikely. By that move the United States has, as we saw earlier, made itself appear the ally of South Africa, Savimbi's other main backer: a development which not only damages the chances of a settlement in Namibia, but, by antagonising all the states of the region, gravely imperils the Western position throughout Southern Africa. Yet there is no sign that it consulted its allies before taking that step.

Here too, therefore, it is by no means sure that the United

States is the country best equipped to play the dominant role in securing a settlement. Here too Europe has a historical connection. And here too Europe may have a useful part to play — and should perhaps have been more actively involved in the negotiation process from the beginning. At the very least it should be more actively seeking to influence a US policy which is potentially so damaging to the West as a whole. But unless, here too, the Community abandons the self-effacing posture which it and its individual members have adopted over the past few years, it is unlikely that its views will have much influence.

Another area where the Europeans have a traditional connection is South-East Asia. France has had links for over a century with the countries of Indo-China, links which have not been totally effaced by recent events; while Britain has had even more long-standing ties, admittedly weakening, with Malaysia and Singapore. It cannot be said, however, that over the last few years Europe has made any substantial input into the solution of the problems of the area. In this region, too, it has taken a back seat. China, the Soviet Union and the United States are now the dominant external powers. Most European countries have continued to back the United States in supporting the fanciful claims to Cambodia's UN seat of the so-called "coalition", which now controls virtually no Cambodian territory, is bitterly divided between its three component parts, and is dominated by the clique of the murderous Pol Pot. They have made little or no effort to prevent the United States from translating this political support for the coalition, in co-operation with China, into overt military support for attacks across the Cambodian frontier, though this self-evidently makes much harder the achievement of the West's professed goal, the withdrawal of Vietnam. That policy is not only dubious on grounds of principle but also politically misguided, since it can only push Vietnam, and Cambodia with it, further and further into the arms of the Soviet Union: the reverse of what the West claims to wish for the area. It is parodoxical that there are now some signs that the United States (or at least its State Department) recognises the folly of this policy and is seeking an improved relationship with Vietnam. And it is a sorry commentary on Europe's current "me too" role that it may now eventually belatedly follow along behind the United States in this changed approach, when, given Europe's historical ties, it might — if not so intent on a low posture — have taken the lead in promoting a more sensible approach to the area's problems.

Central America is not a region with which most of Europe can claim historical ties; and it is certainly one where it must recognise a far stronger US interest. Yet, here too, Europe is entitled to a view, and to make it known, as tactfully but effectively as possible, to the US administration. One reason for this is that the policy the United States is now pursuing in that area — that of giving active assistance to rebels seeking to overthrow a government which it, as well as the Community countries, recognises — represents only one component in a set of similar policies being adopted in many parts of the world. It is a policy which Western states loudly and consistently condemned in the past when they believed it was being pursued by Communist states who were giving assistance to rebels in Greece, China, Vietnam, Cambodia, and Bolivia and other Latin American states, for example. And it is a policy which, if it once more became the norm, would lead to a chronically unstable international society, in which rival interventions were habitually undertaken in any of the hundred-or-so less democratic countries of the world (even assuming it was confined to less democratic states).

If European countries are unhappy about the long-term consequences of such a policy, they have not only the right but the duty to make those views known. So far the only protests they appear to have made have been those which were purely self-interested, as against American moves to mine Nicaraguan ports in spring 1984. But the fact is that current US policies, if maintained and intensified as currently seems to be happening, could be seriously damaging to the West as a whole, as well as to the United States. They tend to identify the West with a policy of assisting external attacks against the territory of another state; with support for generally reactionary forces (such as the followers of the Somoza family and Pol Pot); with great-power bullying; and with the crude effort to use military means to solve what are essentially political problems. They risk endangering the West's political position throughout the areas where they are practised (for example, in Latin America and Southern Africa). Above all they are policies which, most observers agree, have little chance of finally prevailing and could therefore ultimately cause substantial loss of face to the West as a whole. Europe thus has every justification, even in terms of Western interest, in speaking its mind more loudly on such questions than it has in the past.

Arms control and defence

But perhaps the area where Europe's failure to play an active role is most visible and most damaging is that of arms control. Over recent years it has been taken for granted that negotiations on nuclear-arms reduction are undertaken by the super-powers alone. Even if the negotiations were confined to strategic weapons, this would be somewhat odd, since the British and French nuclear forces, as the Soviet Union consistently claims, clearly have some strategic role. But in fact the negotiations also concern intermediate weapons, which more obviously include the British and French nuclear armouries. The practical disadvantages of leaving out Britain and France are already visible. Soviet demands for an undertaking that Britain and France should agree not to increase their present nuclear capabilities have become a key element in the negotiations; but it is one that had to be covered by correspondence outside the framework of the negotiations themselves.

The absence of European participation does not affect only the nuclear powers of Europe. Any arms-control agrement reached between the super-powers must have a very direct effect on their allies: possibly, even, a more decisive effect than on themselves (since neither is likely to bargain away its own minimum deterrent force, while they might be tempted to agree reductions which have a major influence on the balance in Europe). The concern about the "decoupling" of Europe from the United States, or about the possibility that the strategic defence iniative (SDI) could leave Europe exposed while the United States was (or believed itself to be) protected, reflects this interdependence.

For all these reasons, Europe should be able to present its viewpoint on such questions in a more direct way than it can today. Of course there is already consultation, a great deal of it, on the position the United States should adopt in the negotiations. But in Europe's eyes this is often inadequate to protect its interests. An almost comic example occurred when the United States, in response to what were believed to be European attitudes, moved back towards the "zero option" position, only to find, after it had announced this publicly, that the Europeans had decided that they did not like it after all. There could be no clearer demonstration that the current procedures for consultation on such questions are inadequate, and certainly no substitute for direct participation.

There are, admittedly, very real difficulties about providing Europe with a direct voice. In the face of their widely differing interests, how easily could the Europeans arrive at a common position? Again, if Europe, separately represented, gave a different point of view from the United States, would this not present to the world the spectacle of a divided West, offering an opportunity to the Soviet Union for deliberately exploiting disunity? In fact, each of these difficulties already exists under the present system. Even if they are only to be consulted, rather than separately represented, the Europeans need to formulate a position; and a joint West European position is certainly no harder to arrive at than a joint Western position, such as is at present necessary. Similarly, the Soviet Union will seek to exploit apparent differences of position and interest between the United States and Europe anyway, and already does so; and it would not automatically find it easier to do this if Europe were separately represented in the negotiations. In fact, for the first 20 years or so after 1945 there was separate representation for four Western countries (the United States, Britain, France and Canada) in the principal negotiations concerning disarmament; and they normally had no difficulty in presenting a united front. There is no self-evident reason why it should be harder to reach agreed negotiating positions today if there were only two main Western participants, the United States and the Community.

However, at present the situation is even worse than this,

since there is not even any significant degree of consultation on
the main strategic *decisions*. The US decision to embark upon
the SDI has had a decisive effect on the prospects for nuclear
disarmament and on the entire strategic balance between East
and West. It will have a major impact on Europe, since the
defence policies of European countries may have to be significantly modified to take account of it. This applies equally to
the US decision to abandon SALT II, which will equally affect
Europe. Yet there is no evidence that any consultation with
West European countries took place before these decisions
were announced; and the opportunity for those countries to
dissent (which almost all of them have done) came only after
they had already been presented with a *fait accompli*. This
might again be seen as a reason why Western Europe — that is,
in practice, the European Community — should seek recognition as an equal partner (or nearly equal) in the process of
negotiations on nuclear weapons, rather than continuing to
rely on the inadequate consultation which takes place at present. And it is especially odd that France and Britain, themselves nuclear powers, if minor ones, have been content for so
long to be relegated to the insignificant role which they at
present occupy in these vital negotiations.

In defence, because of the varying positions and interests of
the members, the problem is more complex. There have been
divisions in the past between those members of the Community
that were nuclear powers and those that were not; those that
were members of the Nuclear Planning Group and those outside; those, such as France, that were not members of the
integrated NATO system, and those that were; those that did
and those that did not have signficant US forces on their soil;
large powers and small; and so on. Some members of NATO
were within the Community, and as many outside. Some were
members of the West European Union, and others were not.

With the enlargement of the Community these difficulties
have been somewhat reduced. Of the European members of
NATO, only Norway and Turkey are now outside the Community (and the latter at least has associate status). Conversely,
of the 12 members of the Community, only Ireland is not also a
member of NATO. This makes it more realistic than

before for the Community to begin, as many have suggested, to play a role in the field of defence. In the recent agreement on foreign policy co-ordination, it was laid down that "closer co-operation on questions of European security will contribute in an essential way to the development of a European external identity". It remains to be seen how this will be put into effect. Certainly if Europe's view is to acquire any influence on such questions as defence procurement and the need for a "two-way street" in the flow of contracts between Europe and the United States, nuclear strategy, naval policy in the Mediterranean and the Black Sea, the SDI, and other questions of direct interest to Europe, it will become increasingly necessary for it to be possible to formulate a common European view.

As the credibility of the US nuclear umbrella declines (a decline that the development of the SDI has hastened) there is increasing recognition, in Western Europe as in Britain, of the vital importance of a purely European nuclear capability if credible deterrence against a localised threat in Europe is to be maintained. This will create the desire among the non-nuclear states to be able to influence the nuclear policies of their fellow members which have that capability. Thus the step which, more than any other, might improve defence co-operation in Europe would be one which reduced the wide gulf which at present divides the nuclear from the non-nuclear powers. The most important such step would be for Britain and France to engage in far wider discussions with each other and with their Community partners about their policies relating to their nuclear forces. There should be regular consultation on such questions as nuclear strategy, deployment and targeting. Even if there ultimately remained, as seems inevitable, only a single finger (or two fingers) on the trigger, increasingly it would be Western Europe rather than France or Britain individually that was perceived as the unit possessing a nuclear capability. Eventually it is not impossible that, if only for symbolic purposes, some degree of joint financing and even joint manning of nuclear submarines might be contemplated. A change of this kind, perhaps more than anything else, might make a reality of European co-operation on defence questions. It could thus cause Europe increasingly to be seen as an integrated unit which, by virtue of its nuclear capability, must inevitably have a major part to play in the discussion of world affairs.

Finding a collective voice for Europe

Whether or not a more equal partnership is to come about — and it is probably not an immediate prospect — if Europe is to be able to play a more direct part in the discussion of world issues, both in foreign affairs and defence, the first prerequisite is clearly that it should be better able than at present to formulate a collective view of its own. Though foreign policy is not covered in the Treaty of Rome, there have been attempts for some years to secure a common Community viewpoint on major questions through the system of European "political co-operation". Regular consultations take place at a number of different levels: six-monthly summits, regular meetings of foreign ministers, including private weekends from time to time; meetings of Community ambassadors in Brussels; and many meetings of specialists in different fields — the Middle East, Southern Africa, the United Nations, and so on — attended by senior officials from each capital, also usually in Brussels. Through these means an attempt is made to bring the policies of individual member states closer together.

The recent reform of the Community, which included an agreement for improved co-operation on foreign policy, will marginally strengthen but will not fundamentally transform that system. Under the new arrangements, members have undertaken to "inform and consult each other on any foreign policy matters". "Common principles and objectives" will be gradually developed and defined. Foreign ministers will meet four times a year. And a secretariat in Brussels will help the state holding the presidency of the European Council to co-ordinate foreign policy.

The political co-operation process has probably already had more impact than the public realises, especially on the details of policy. At the very least, it has produced far greater mutual understanding between European governments. Fewer differences of view are visible on most foreign affairs questions now than, for example, in the days of General de Gaulle, even perhaps of Willy Brandt and Harold Wilson. When major differences do arise today, they tend to be those expressed by smaller member countries, such as Greece, rather than larger states such as Germany, France, Britain or Italy. Between these there is on most major issues usually some affinity of view.

The difficulty today lies not so much in a diversity of views among the European states as in the lack of any platform from which to express those views. The assumption of bipolarity has left Europe, in the eyes of the world, as a kind of appendage of the United States rather than an independent actor on the world's stage. Europe today is, almost as much as Japan, taken for granted; and, like Japan, Europe therefore plays a role far too slight for its real weight, whether measured in economic strength, military power, population or diplomatic experience and expertise. One reason is, of course, that for many purposes the Community still constitutes a collection of individual states, each of which is a relatively insignificant power by modern standards, rather than being seen and treated as a collective unit.

This weakness could to some extent be remedied if there existed a single figure who, at least on major questions, could speak for the Community as a whole. This happens to a limited extent at the annual economic summits. There the Community is represented by the President of the Commission, who attends in addition to the representatives of its major states. There may be other occasions when the President could represent, even speak for, the Community as a whole: sometimes even instead of the member states rather than in addition to them. In more specialised areas, commissioners, especially the Commissioner for External Affairs or the commissioner most closely involved with the subject concerned, could play a similar role; and this would above all be the case where there was a clear Community competence (as, for example, on fishing questions).

But more effective, perhaps, in establishing the image of the Community as a single unit with a weight comparable to its effective power would be a convention that the *government* which currently exercised the presidency would represent the

Community on important foreign affairs questions. In negotiations on trade, for example (which is entirely within Community competence), on defence, disarmament, or environmental
questions, and even in informal discussions, whether with the
United States, the Soviet Union, China or Japan, that government might on appropriate occasions speak for the Community
as a whole. At the Conference on the Law of the Sea a joint
statement was often read out on behalf of the Community as a
whole, representing a Community position; thus, at least in
theory, the Community might have been represented there by
a single state rather than by nine or ten, of which only one
spoke. At present, *joint* representations by the ambassadors of
all Community states are sometimes made. But with the recent
enlargement of the Community this has become an increasingly
cumbersome system. The expression of the Community view
by a single voice, both publicly and privately, on appropriate
occasions, might do more than anything else to give it a weight
in world affairs comparable to the power which it collectively
wields.

Europe today is almost in the position which the United
States held before 1914: a political force of substantial power,
whose voice is none the less scarcely heard on the world scene.
Since 1914, after 30 or so years of coexistence, the US voice has
become progressively louder, while that of Europe is now
scarcely audible at all. But Europe too has something worth
saying on the great issues of the day. The dialogue on those
questions should no longer be monopolised by the super-
powers.

The time has come to call in the old world to redress the
balance of the new.

7 The Changing United Nations

It is not only better understandings among the super-powers, and a more clearly acknowledged role for other important power centres, that will be needed if a more stable international society is to be established. There will also be a need for a revitalised and a more effective United Nations.

The changes described in earlier chapters have affected that organisation too. A body that was created to deal with overt acts of "aggression" finds itself instead faced with various forms of intervention and other more indirect and ambiguous uses of armed force. A body expected to confront conflicts across frontiers confronts instead conflicts which overwhelmingly take place within them. A body of 50 member states, expected to operate democratically, has been replaced by one of 160, confronting a world in which power is increasingly concentrated in two dominant super-states. It is a commonplace that the United Nations today does not fulfil the task within contemporary international society that its founders planned for it. Before considering what needs to be done if the United Nations is to play a more effective part in the future it may be worth examining the various reasons why the role which the United Nations plays today is so different from that which was originally hoped.

First, the Charter was based on the assumption that though, on matters *directly* affecting themselves, the permanent members would be able to prevent UN action through the use of the veto, there would be a wide range of other matters on which they would normally be able to agree on the type of action required. The common belief that the founders of the United Nations assumed "great-power unanimity" is an absurdity: the cold war had already begun at the time the Charter was signed in 1945 and few were so naïve as to think that there would not be serious disagreement on many of the matters which arose. The veto was precisely designed to act as a safety valve so that the effect of disagreement was not to smash the machine irreparably. What is true is that the shrinkage of distance, in strategic terms, made the disagreements far more all-pervading than expected. It was soon discovered that there was no part of the world, however remote, which was not seen as essential to their interests by some or all of the great powers. The result was that over Iran (1946) as over Lebanon (1958), over the Middle East as over Indo-China, over Central America as over Southern Africa, the organisation was split fatally. Over Vietnam, for ten years the world's most important trouble-spot, the United Nations was almost totally inactive, largely for that reason. Today there are very few issues, wherever they arise, on which there is not a major conflict of interest between the permanent members; and this often prevents effective action from being taken in the United Nations.

Second, a very large proportion of conflict situations in the modern world are, at least nominally, internal problems. Most wars in the contemporary world, as we saw earlier, are civil wars rather than international wars (or at least begin as such). Over such questions Article 2(7) of the Charter, prohibiting interference in matters that are "essentially within the domestic jurisdiction" of a member state, can be used to prevent UN action. In some cases, as over the Congo and Cyprus, the government concerned actively demanded a UN role. But other domestic wars (such as Biafra, Western Sahara, Sri Lanka and the long-standing conflicts in Burma, Ethiopia, Sudan, Chad, Mozambique, and the Philippines — in other words many of the main conflict situations of recent years) have not been considered at all. It seems reasonable to forecast that conflicts in the next decade or two will continue to be predominantly of this type. Unless there is a new willingness to bring them to the United Nations, the organisation may continue inactive over most of the conflicts of the day.

Third, the increasingly explicit acceptance of recognised spheres of influence has also weakened the United Nations' role. The West has not attempted to interfere in Eastern Europe: even when armed force was used in Hungary and Czechoslovakia. The Soviet Union was prepared to accept the dominance of the United States over the affairs of Guatemala (1954) and the Dominican Republic (1965) and, ultimately, in the Cuban missile crisis: and has taken only a marginal interest in the affairs of Central America generally. The growth of Western European and Chinese power, the increasing resentment in Africa and Latin America at great-power interference, may create new, more limited spheres of influence. Eventually there may emerge a world of continental regions, each concerned to regulate its own affairs. Within each region dominant powers may become increasingly reluctant to tolerate ouside intervention, even by the United Nations. Where there are regional organisations, such as the Organisation of American States (OAS), the Organisation of African Unity (OAU) and the emerging European institutions, these may be held to have the primary role in solving local problems and disputes. The United Nations may thus be increasingly marginalised.

Fourth, a considerable number of the major issues of the modern world are questions of human rights, whether the rights are those of individuals (say in Southern Africa or the Soviet Union) or of large minorities (such as the Kurds in Turkey, Iraq and Iran, the Eritreans and Tigreans in Ethiopia, the peoples of East Timor and Western Sahara). The United Nations is a body of nation states, however, each concerned to preserve national sovereignty; and each probably having at least one human-rights skeleton in its own cupboard. The assembled governments within that organisation therefore, of which few are deeply concerned over human-rights issues, are reluctant to interfere too blatantly in the internal affairs of another state. Thus, when the provisions of Article 2(7) are invoked by the governments accused, they are interpreted with some sympathy and understanding by other members. Where the violation is a particularly gross one, and where there is a large number of nations which feel strong solidarity with the oppressed group (as over South Africa), such objections may be overcome. In other cases, even where basic political rights are undoubtedly denied, there is often a reluctance to offend a fellow government by taking too strong a line.

Fifth, some of the great powers oppose a strong UN role. The Communist countries in general, as a permanent minority group within the United Nations, and one pathologically suspicious of all external interference, have always been apprehensive that the organisation could be used against their interests by the majority (its present Afro-Asian majority as much as its former Western majority). For this reason they have been consistently hostile to any steps which might have the effect of strengthening the organisation. They have opposed increases in the organisation's budget and those of the agencies. They have opposed "strong" candidates for Secretary-General. They are unfavourable to any extension of the United Nations' peace-keeping role, as well as anything else which looks even remotely "supranational". Today the United States too is increasingly cautious in its approach, and is actively seeking to reduce its financial commitment. Britain and France are little more positive. The permanent members have even combined together to urge a slower rate of growth in the organisation's annual budget, recently securing a virtual veto on this. This symbolises their general distaste for international authority.

Sixth, the fact that a large proportion of the membership is made up of very small countries, exercising equal voting power with the very largest, weakens UN authority. The fact that majority votes in the Assembly can now be passed by 100 governments representing well under 10 per cent of the world's population, against the will of 10 or 12 nations representing 90 per cent, makes its resolutions increasingly unrepresentative. It arouses resentment. It lessens respect for UN resolutions. And it makes the largest powers particularly chary of giving any effective authority to the organisation, especially to its Assembly. It is true, and is often forgotten, that Assembly resolutions are only recommendations anyway, and should be taken as simply an expression of opinion. But even in the Security Council, whose resolutions can have mandatory force, the criticism has some validity. When, as sometimes occurs, half the members of the Council are very small states, it is not surprising that the largest countries regard its resolutions with less than total veneration.

Seventh, the development of super-power politics — bilateral dealings between the United States and the Soviet Union, and now increasingly between both those states and China — as a means of resolving important issues, accentuates this downgrading of the United Nations. Not only do the big powers look less to the United Nations to solve their problems; they have new channels of their own which can replace it. So a form of "by-passing" develops. The feeling grows that the major issues will *only* be decided through such channels. And once again the United Nations begins to appear irrelevant.

Eighth, the somewhat disappointing record over questions of peace and war over the last 10 or 20 years is cumulative in effect. Most are aware that a large number of wars take place, almost entirely uninfluenced by the organisation. Few people any longer expect the United Nations to be able to deal with such matters effectively. This itself encourages efforts to solve such problems outside the United Nations. Countries which are themselves threatened or attacked become more sceptical about the value of turning to the United Nations for assistance. This too, together with continuing financial problems (which inhibit new peace-keeping operations), promotes disillusion.

Ninth, the increasingly glaring economic disparities between rich countries and poor create pressures and tensions of a new kind, which the United Nations has not yet found a means of resolving. To the rich countries the United Nations, with its associated agencies, begins to look more and more like a glorified begging bowl, directing ever more onerous demands towards them. To the poor, it seems to provide an increasingly inadequate response to the many legitimate claims they make upon it. Either way, images of the United Nations and of its proper role increasingly diverge, and become the source of more and more misunderstandings.

Finally, and perhaps most fundamental of all, the old Adam of national sovereignty will not go away as obligingly as the United Nations' founders hoped. Nationalist feeling, in some parts of the world at least, becomes more powerful than ever. Governments that are strongly influenced by these sentiments do not easily respond to the urgings of an international organisation, which in any case has no ultimate means of enforcing its wishes. Most governments support the United Nations where the UN view is identical with their own. Just as the West could make a virtue of supporting it in the first 20 years, when what the United Nations wanted was what the West wanted, so now the Afro-Asians can present themselves as powerful supporters of the United Nations, since what it wants means what they want. Where the United Nations' wishes conflict with those of individual nations, however, there is little it can do to enforce conformity. Most nations, third-world as much as Western or Communist, are not yet ready to surrender any significant part of their independence of action to an international organisation; and especially not on the basic questions of peace and war where this surrender is most necessary. So Indonesia defies the organisation in East Timor; Morocco in Western Sahara; Vietnam in Cambodia; as blatantly as the Soviet Union in Afghanistan and the US in Nicaragua. A wide variety of states continue to violate the human rights of their populations, regardless of the exhortations and injunctions of the United Nations. The pleadings of the majority are thus unable to exercise any influence where important questions of national interest are believed to be at stake.

The erosion of military power, therefore, in changing the character of international society, has also changed the environment within which the United Nations operates. But the difficulty that individual states have in making their power effective does not automatically mean that it is easier for the United Nations itself to exercise authority. On the contrary, it too is unable to use or threaten the use of force, if necessary, as its founders intended, to maintain world peace. It too is obliged to consider ways of exercising authority by influence and persuasion rather than by the collective use of force; by political rather than military means. It too therefore needs to consider alternative means to expand its authority and activity in the type of international environment that now exists.

Implications for the future

All of these difficulties are real ones, and there is nothing to be gained by blinking them. In considering how the United

Nations could or should evolve in the future, it is necessary to bear them constantly in mind. It is worth examining each in turn to consider the implications they have for the United Nations' future.

First, the fact that in the modern world events in any part are felt to be of vital importance to each super-power does not necessarily mean that the United Nations is made helpless. It certainly means that there will be no easily mobilised five-power consensus, such as is sometimes said to have been foreseen when the United Nations was created, even on events in deepest Asia, or darkest Latin America. Such agreement will normally have to be manufactured. Each power will have its own views, its own interests, its own client governments to defend, its own face to save. What this means is that agreed solutions will only come about by careful and patient *negotiation* to secure them. The United Nations can still act effectively where it works on the basis of such negotiations, rather than knee-jerk reactions and public gestures.

Second, the fact that so many conflicts are internal does not in itself preclude a UN role. A considerable number of civil-war situations have in fact been discussed by the United Nations since its foundation: those in Greece, Laos, Yemen, Congo, Cyprus and Lebanon among others. Peace forces were sent in the last three cases, and observers in the others. Representatives of the Secretary-General sought to resolve civil conflicts in the Dominican Republic, and to perform humanitarian roles in Biafra and Bangladesh. Where no attempt has been made to involve the United Nations in internal conflicts, this is not always because of the resistance of the government chiefly concerned. Often it is simply because no outside government has ever thought to raise the matter; or because some other government has objected to its being discussed. If outside countries had been more persistent in asking for discussion (for example, of the war in Guatemala in 1954 or of that in Nigeria between 1968 and 1970, above all of the war in Vietnam), those questions might well have been debated. Since external interference was an important factor in many civil wars (for example Vietnam, El Salvador, Nicaragua, Chad and Angola), it is astonishing that they are not more discussed. In practice, however, outside countries have usually been cautious, to the point of timidity, in seeking to raise issues of this kind. Yet even in a civil conflict the United Nations can promote or encourage negotiations among the parties, or set in train some form of mediation. Since civil wars are, as we have seen, a substantial proportion of all wars, and since there is in many cases external intervention, it is clearly absurd that, over recent years at least, these are precisely the conflicts it avoids discussing.

Third, the increasingly explicit acceptance of spheres of influence, though it certainly creates some problems, can in other ways make the United Nations' role more important. The benefit (if any) of the sphere-of-influence concept is that it may discourage distant super-powers from interfering in areas where they have no overriding interest. Its danger is that it may *encourage* the nearest super-power to interfere in such a zone, in the confident expectation that all other major powers will keep their hands off. This is what happened in Hungary and Guatemala, in the Dominican Republic and Czechoslovakia. Even regional organisations cannot act as a useful counter-force in such situations if they are themselves dominated by the super-power concerned, or by an ideological majority hostile to a minority state: this has largely destroyed the capacity of the OAS or the Warsaw Pact to meet such situations. It thus becomes all the more essential for the United Nations to be available as a long stop, or an umpire, to be appealed to if necessary by a small nation which feels it has not received fair play from the regional organisation concerned. Though the United Nations may reasonably call on a regional body to examine a particular dispute or to act on its behalf in the first place, it must retain the ultimate responsibility if those efforts fail.

Fourth, the dominance of human-rights issues creates difficult but not insuperable problems. At first sight there is a basic conflict between the human-rights provisions of the Charter, asserting the United Nations' interest in this field, and the provisions of Article 2(7) excluding interference in questions "essentially within the domestic jurisdiction" of member states. A reading of the Charter as a whole, however, makes it clear that the former provisions prevail over the latter: indeed, there would have been no point in inserting any human-rights provisions at all if it was intended that any future Hitler would be enabled to set about massacring millions of his own population in the confident knowledge that he could exclude UN interest by invoking this article. Moreover, the judgement of what issues are "essentially within the domestic jurisdiction" of member states is itself a subjective one; and one which, as the International Court has pointed out, varies from one generation to another. It is the caution of the membership rather than the provisions of the Charter which has inhibited more widespread discussion of such issues. Even the Human Rights Commission, which was set up precisely for this purpose, has, until recently, avoided discussing specific violations of human rights, as against general principles. For similar reasons, the proposal for a High Commissioner for Human Rights, which has been raised regularly in the General Assembly for many years, has consistently been talked out. If the United Nations wishes to increase the respect in which it is held and to appear to take seriously the commitments contained in the Charter, it will need to develop and extend its activities in this area. The process of drafting wide and woolly conventions and declarations affirming impeccable good intentions in this field, to which governments will gladly put their names whatever their real intentions, has now gone as far as it reasonably can. The time has come for the United Nations to turn to implementation: measures to ensure that the standards laid down are being effectively maintained (as has for years been done with considerable effectiveness in the human rights operations of the Council of Europe).

Fifth, the negative attitude of the Soviet bloc and some other powers in the United Nations towards the strengthening of international authority is not being modified. The Soviet Union has agreed to pay peacekeeping costs. But it remains unlikely that any changes in the system will come about through Charter revision. The Soviet Union has made clear its opposition to any attempt to introduce amendments to the Charter (other than purely nominal changes — for example, in the size of various UN bodies) or even to hold a review conference, on the grounds that the present Charter is the best it could possibly expect to get. Other permanent members are almost equally cautious. This does not, however, mean that no other changes in the UN structure or procedures can be introduced. Significant reforms can be made, including an improvement in the United Nations' peace-keeping capacity, without any formal amendment of the Charter. Already changes in procedure (the acceptance that an abstention in the Security Council does not represent a veto, the development of the United Nations' economic role, the establishment of new Assembly committees, and the development of peace-keeping forces) have come about without changes in the Charter. A great deal more could be done in the same way.

Sixth, it is inevitable that respect for Assembly resolutions among large powers, where the majority that passes them consists largely of very small states, must decline. The often-proposed solution, the introduction of a system of weighted voting, is attractive but unlikely to be implemented. The majority of over-represented small states are hardly likely to sign away their present privileged position with a stroke of the pen. Nor would even the basic principles of any such scheme be at all easy to agree. Would it be based on population, on contributions to the United Nations, on gross national product, or what? Each of these obviously bristles with difficulties of one kind or another (such as giving huge power to China on the one hand, or the United States on the other). The most likely solution would be the introduction of some kind of additional, or bonus, votes for the largest powers. The Soviet Union in effect already has three votes in the General Assembly (through the representation of the Ukraine and Byelo-Russia). The United States, China and India might be given three votes by a similar device, while countries with populations of 20–150 million might have two. But even this is a very doubtful starter. In fact, the number voting for Assembly resolutions is of far less importance than is sometimes believed. There is much to be said for devoting far less time to the discussion of resolutions, as at present, and far more to the negotiation of settlements. The important thing would then not be to force through votes by a bare majority, but to negotiate solutions acceptable to the states most concerned and, if possible, to the major powers and groups within the membership. Indeed, the one advantage that may come from the increasing number of very small states is that less and less importance is likely to be attached to resolutions unless they secure the consent of the powers directly involved, and especially of the larger powers of the international community.

Seventh, the cumulative effect of the United Nations' failure to solve earlier disputes cannot be altogether undone. It is already the case that there is less readiness to turn immediately to the United Nations for the answer whenever a conflict occurs anywhere. The one bonus from this is that somewhat less exacting standards may come to be demanded. If it becomes more widely accepted that in many situations the United Nations can act, if at all, only to promote and encourage negotiation, not only will less be hoped of it, but there will be less reason to fear UN "interference" among the parties to disputes. There may then be a willingness to turn to the organisation more often. This would demand some changes in the United Nations' own procedures. For example, the Security Council should view its own role rather differently. By assuming whenever it meets that its first and main task it to pass a resolution, it wastes precious hours in negotiating the exact terms of a document that may have little impact on the outcome and be forgotten in a week. By concentrating more on the idea of *mediation*, of bringing the parties together, even without a formal resolution being passed, the Council could enhance its role. By failing, in the case of the Middle East, to bring about any effective negotiation between the parties over 20 or 30 years, even indirectly, it has in effect denied itself any influence on the outcome altogether, and reduced the influence that Resolution 242 (which each party — other than the PLO — eventually accepted) might otherwise have had on the situation. Similarly, if, over Vietnam the organisation had sought simply to promote negotiations, rather than to pass judgement in the form of resolutions, objections to a UN role might have been less strenuous.

Eighth, the development of super-power politics, while it complicates the role of the United Nations, need not eliminate it. On many issues there is scope for both bilateral and multi-lateral discussion. The latter can sometimes provide the framework and the guidelines for the former. Third-party influence is brought to bear, at least on questions of general principle. But the details can still be left to the parties themselves to resolve between them. Super-power diplomacy makes this third-party influence more, not less, important. Without it, the major issues of the day would be resolved by the great powers, over the heads of many smaller ones which may be intimately affected by the result. Small powers would then feel increasingly that they were simply pawns and puppets, dependent on the doings and dealings of the great with each other. The discussion of such issues as disarmament, Central America and Afghanistan within the wider framework, as well as the narrower, may help to remind the larger powers of the need to take careful heed of smaller countries which have an interest, and so a right to a say, in the outcome.

Ninth, the increasing economic confrontation between rich countries and poor is another of those realities which must be reflected in the UN looking-glass. Because the issue has become the most important confrontation of modern world society, it inevitably exerts an even greater impact than most on the politics of the United Nations. North–South polarisation takes place on very many questions that are not exclusively economic: the environment, the budgets of the specialised agencies, the authority to be attributed to international law, and so on. One effect is that on such questions the United States and the Soviet Union are increasingly brought together on the same side. But the North–South confrontation need not inhibit the effectiveness of the United Nations in questions of peace and war. It increases the need, as always when large blocks are involved, for objectivity by members of each group when issues affecting one of their number arise. At present, alignments of other kinds, ideological, regional or historical, are still sufficiently significant to prevent polarisation on the economic basis alone. Here once more, however, the existence of two interest groups, coming into conflict with each other over a whole range of issues, underlines the need for more effective *negotiating* procedures for discussing such questions.

Tenth, the persistence of the demands of national sovereignty is the difficulty least easily brushed aside. This is the problem perhaps most basic to the purposes of the United Nations and its potential for peace. Governments still, in general, favour international action when it promotes their own country's interests, but resist it when the reverse is the case. Since they are *national* governments, it could scarcely be otherwise. And, since they know that in the final resort the United Nations cannot enforce its demands, they will probably continue to ignore them when this suits their convenience. This is the real challenge which the United Nations faces. It does not, at present, and will not for the foreseeable future, possess superior *power* to that available to its members. It must therefore depend for the extension of its authority on the development of its *influence*. This is not necessarily impossible. But it requires somewhat more sophisticated methods and techniques than those which have been adopted in the past. It would require the development of a coherent set of principles of national behaviour to be applied consistently in considering the issues coming before the organisation. It would require scrupulous objectivity in applying these principles and rules to individual cases, regardless of national, regional or ideological interests. It would need new techniques of mediation, conciliation and dispute settlement not yet adequately developed. It might also require UN authority to be enhanced in a number of economic and functional fields, where political antipathies and tensions are less serious and the need for international action is more widely recognised (see Chapter 8 below).

These are not easy goals to achieve. But by these means the authority of the United Nations might gradually be built up, in such a way that it will finally be able to make headway against the stubborn resistances of national sovereignty.

The limits of UN power

In considering the way the United Nations could develop over the next decade and the action that member governments could best take to promote reform, it is esssential to distinguish clearly between what the organisation can reasonably be ex-

pected to do, given the existing state of international relationships, and what it cannot; in other words, to take careful
account of the *limits* to its power. Only by clearly recognising
these limits, will it be possible at the same time to identify
those areas where it can acquire a more effective role.

First, the United Nations cannot normally stop a war once it
has already broken out. The belief that it should be able to do
this, and the disappointment when it does not, is another
example of the unrealistic expectations which have done so
much to breed disillusion with the organisation. It is futile to
expect that, in a situation where fighting is already taking
place, the United Nations has only to issue a call for a cease-
fire, to pass a resolution, or to make other imploring noises, to
bring instant peace. There have been a few occasions where
such calls have, in fact, been followed relatively rapidly by a
cessation of hostilities: over the Arab–Israeli war of 1948, the
Suez war of 1956, the India–Pakistan war of 1965, and the
Israeli–Arab war of 1967, resolutions of the Council or Assembly demanding a cease-fire were accepted and rapidly complied
with (though it would be rash to assume that the cease-fire was
simply a *result* of the UN resolutions). These are, however, not
entirely typical, and there have been many other cases, especially in recent times, where such calls have been ignored.
Sometimes in such situations the United Nations, though it
cannot immediately halt a war, can initiate actions which later
lead to a settlement: appoint a mediator, call a conference, or
promote negotiations under the auspices of the Secretary-
General. The more obvious conclusion, however, is that the
United Nations must seek to influence disputes *before* they
reach the stage of conflict. Once war breaks out, the United
Nations has already failed. Yet in a large proportion of the
cases in which wars have occurred in recent years, the organisation had made virtually no attempt even to consider the dispute
before conflict erupted. If the United Nations is invariably
called in only after wars have broken out, it is scarcely surprising if it is regarded as a permanent failure.

Second, the United Nations cannot in most cases impose
settlements on the basis of a majority vote on unwilling dis-
putants, whether big powers or small. It can lead the horses to

the water, but it cannot compel them to drink the peace potions offered, if they are determined not to do so. In certain cases the United Nations can set out the general *guidelines* which it believes should be applied in a settlement; this is what the Security Council did in its Resolution 242 on the Middle East. It can appoint a *mediator* to seek to promote such a settlement; as it did in the same case and over Kashmir, Cyprus, the Gulf War, Afghanistan and other conflicts. Occasionally, on matters of fundamental importance it can impose *sanctions,* economic or otherwise, to bring about the implementation of the particular solution it has endorsed — as it did over Rhodesia. In most cases, however, its task will be to encourage and facilitate, rather than to impose, settlements.

Third, it is unrealistic to hope that the United Nations can "solve" basic disputes, especially among the major powers. Here too it will *reflect* reality, rather than remoulding it altogether. What the organisation can do in such cases is to provide the *channels* through which such divisions can be discussed. It can secure greater understanding of the positions and interests of others, and a point of contact and communication for discussing them. However, if the United Nations is to replace alternative means of resolving conflicts, the channels it provides must be private as well as public. Where, as at present, communication (on the substance of disputes, as opposed to the terms of resolutions) is largely public — in meetings of the Security Council, for example — it is used mainly for condemnation and abuse; and a dispute is more likely to be intensified than resolved in this way. If the United Nations is really to be able to pacify the underlying conflicts, it must be able to provide informal and private channels of communication to supplement those which take place in the debating chamber (see p. 176 below).

A fourth and more obvious limitation to the United Nations' power concerns its capacity to enforce its will in internal matters. Much UN action is directed at influencing the policies of member states in their own territories: for example, on civil conflicts, or in seeking to secure better respect for human rights (as in calling for an end to the policies of apartheid in South Africa). The effectiveness of such action depends ultimately on its being able to influence the general climate of opinion, both within the state concerned and elsewhere. This in turn depends on the extent to which resolutions appear representative of widespread opinion. But it also depends on their realism and credibility. If, for example, they threaten sanctions which important members are not prepared to fulfil, or make demands far beyond those likely to be met by the state concerned, they may only emphasise the organisation's impotence. Such pressures must therefore be formulated in the form which will be most effective. Every nation and government today is concerned about its image, its place in the world community; and there is no evidence that South Africa, the Soviet Union or any other nation is an exception in this respect. The real weapon the United Nations can utilise over such issues is publicity. The impact it can exert on the internal policies of member states will depend not on the violence of the language employed in its resolutions, but on the effectiveness with which it can publicise demands that enjoy widespread public support. If it can throw the spotlight on flagrant denials of fundamental human rights, wherever they occur, and demonstrate the revulsion such denials cause to most of the rest of humanity, it may be able, even in this field, to exercise some effective influence.

The role the United Nations can perform

If these are the limitations on the United Nations' power, however, it also has assets: things it *can* do, sometimes more effectively than it does today.

First, if the organisation cannot normally stop a war once it has started, it can at least more actively *anticipate* conflict situations before they reach the point of no return. This would require a far greater willingness to initiate discussion in the United Nations, at an early stage, either in formal Council meetings or in informal negotiations about conflict situations. At present, disputes are rarely considered until war has already broken out. In the summer of 1980 tension mounted between Iraq and Iran for several months, and it was obvious that war might shortly break out between them, but no attempt was made to call the Council together. But, once war has broken out, it is already too late. It is not reasonable to expect that in that situation, when passions have been aroused and nations are locked in combat, the Council needs only to issue an imploring plea for a cease-fire or a new negotiation for governments to recall their troops and planes immediately, kiss and make up. The organisation is only likely to be able to act as a constructive influence if it becomes involved in considering disputes at a much earlier stage than it does at present.

Second, even if the United Nations will not normally be in a position to *impose* settlements in international disputes, it could more actively promote negotiations designed to secure them than it has in recent times. This is a technique that has been used by the organisation in the past. Trygve Lie organised fruitful discussions on the Berlin blockade in the UN secretariat in 1949. Dag Hammarskjöld presided at the successful negotiations to formulate the principles of a settlement of the Suez Canal dispute in 1956. This deliberate promotion of private negotiations within the UN building has unfortunately been less often attempted in recent years (though it was tried unsuccessfully over Cyprus in 1984). It might well have produced useful results over the Middle East in the period after 1967, over Bangladesh in 1971, even over the Gulf War and Afghanistan (in place of the inconclusive discussions in which one of the main parties, the Afghan rebels, was unrepresented). Even if the United Nations does not organise such contacts itself, it can call for negotiations among the parties, and provide a point of contact among countries in dispute; and in appropriate cases it can even call a conference to discuss a particular issue (such as that which has been proposed for the Middle East).

Third, the United Nations can, in a much more general way, seek to establish some of the basic preconditions for peaceful relations among states. In a sense it attempts to do this already: by regular consideration of a whole range of issues that divide nations, or are common to all nations, ranging from the seabed to the protein shortage, from population to pollution, from development to drug control. It does so also in the long-term process of codifying international law, which is undertaken by the Sixth Committee of the Assembly and by the International Law Commission. Yet it is arguable that what is required is a more systematic attempt to define a code of conduct in international relations: not so precise or explicit as legal conventions and treaties, nor so vague as the UN Charter, but perhaps more closely related to the realities of the contemporary international system. To take an example: one of the most common types of conflict in the modern world, as we have seen earlier, is that which originates in civil war, but increasingly draws in external powers. Yet the rules concerning external intervention in civil conflicts are among the most hotly disputed within the whole field of international law: the international lawyers of the United States spent 10 years in dispute concerning the legal rights and wrongs of US intervention in Vietnam. A systematic and deliberate effort to formulate more clear-cut rules might do something to reduce the dangers of this type of situation, and act as a more effective inhibition on unilateral action. Similarly, a clearer definition of the situations in which governments are justified in intervening to protect their own nationals abroad might clarify another disputed issue in international law, also occasionally used as a justification for armed action by states. This is only to say that international society, like any other, needs a body of customary rules of interaction amongst its members if the conditions for stable coexistence among states are to be created.

The United Nations is not yet, whatever was once hoped, a world government which can "decide" what nations should do and instruct them accordingly. It cannot yet run the world on the basis of majority votes. It has not yet significantly altered traditional relations among states. What it can do, if properly used, is gradually to *modify* those relations, by maximising the asset which it does possess: *its influence*. It can act as a guide, as a judge, above all as a focus for discussion and contacts. If it uses the authority it possesses in the most effective way, it might eventually bring significant long-term changes in the policies of governments.

Having reviewed the general purposes the organisation should seek to pursue, let us consider in greater detail the changes in its actions and procedures which might make it more effective in its primary role: maintaining world peace.

8 Keeping the Peace

When the United Nations was founded in 1945, it was accepted that its chief task was to keep the peace. Through various procedures for conciliation and peaceful settlement it would try to prevent wars from breaking out in the first place; and, where wars had begun, it would try to bring them to an end quickly, through a system of collective security.

The UN Charter set out two methods by which threats to the peace could be confronted. Chapter VI set out a series of procedures which could be used for resolving disputes before war had occurred: through "negotiation, enquiry, mediation, conciliation, arbitration, judicial settlement, resort to regional agencies or arrangements" (Article 33); "investigation" by the Council (Article 34); consideration by the Security Council or the Assembly (Article 35); the recommendation to the parties concerned of "appropriate procedures or methods of adjustment" by the Security Council (Article 36(1)); and the recommendation by the Security Council, when a dispute was thought likely to endanger international peace and security, of "such terms of settlement as it may consider appropriate" (Article 37).

The second method was set out in Chapter VII. This established the means by which collective enforcement action might be taken to repel aggression if it did occur: the Security Council would call on the parties "to comply with such provisional measures as it deemed necessary or desirable" (Article 40); decide what measures not involving the use of armed force should be employed, including "complete or partial interruption of economic relations, and of rail, sea, air, postal, telegraphic, radio and other means of communication and the severance of diplomatic relations" (Article 41); or "take such action by air, sea or land forces as may be necessary to main-

tain or restore international peace and security" (Article 42).
The system was, in other words, to have been a genuine
collective security system, under which the international community would act together and if necessary join in armed action
against an aggressor if war were to occur.

It soon became apparent that the organisation was unlikely
to be able to use its enforcement powers under Chapter VII.
There are a number of reasons why this was so.

First, the organisation never disposed of the power which
Chapter VII presupposed. Under Article 43 of the Charter all
member states were to contribute armed forces, under agreements concluded between each member and the Security
Council, which could be used by the Council in maintaining
international peace and security. The permanent members
were to negotiate with each other about the precise form this
force should take: the level of sea, land and air forces that
would be required; the extent of the contributions from each
member, in particular from each permanent member; the way
the force would be based and deployed; and how it would be
brought into action. Though such negotiations took place in
1946–7, no agreement could be reached on these points. This
meant that a central premise on which the system was based
was never realised. It was generally believed that, without such
a force, the Council would be unable to "decide" on the use of
force by member states to resist an aggression: decisions
which, under Article 25 of the Charter, would have been
binding on all members. Instead, the Council would have to
rely on "recommendations" to member states to take part in
such actions: recommendations of the kind that occurred when
the Security Council called on member states to come to the
assistance of South Korea when it was attacked in 1950. But
such recommendations could not be binding on any member;
and the fact that in that case only 16 countries contributed,
even in a small way, to the operations of the UN force showed
how limited was the contribution that actions of that kind were
likely to be able to make to the preservation of world peace. In
fact that experiment — the creation of a UN force that was
expected to fight to defend a country under attack — is one
that has never been repeated. As a result the United Nations

has never had coercive power at its disposal. It has lacked the "teeth" with which its founding fathers wished above all to equip it so that it could act more effectively than the League had been able to do to defend the peace.

There was a second reason why enforcement powers could not be used. The veto was more constricting in its effect than had been expected. It was always accepted that the organis-ation would be unable to deal with situations in which the permanent members themselves were closely involved: that is why they were endowed with a veto power to prevent a direct confrontation between the United Nations and any one of them. But, as we saw in the last chapter, it was always assumed that the majority of the situations with which the organisation would deal would not be of this kind. They would be compar-able to those dealt with by the League in its early years: bilateral disputes between small powers unconnected with any of the permanent members. With such questions the organisation should be able to deal effectively, especially if the five perma-nent members, with the considerable power and authority they exercised, were able to agree together on the action required. In practice, after 1945 there proved to be very few questions in which the permanent members, and above all the United States and the Soviet Union, did *not* have an interest. On almost all the questions that emerged in the early years — Iran, Syria and Lebanon, Greece, Indonesia, Palestine, above all Korea — they felt themselves to be closely concerned and took opposite sides. Often this condemned the United Nations to impotence. Permanent members were concerned to prevent decisions from being taken that were contrary to their in-terests. As a result, in many cases effective action, above all enforcement action, was made impossible because of the use of the veto: in the early years mainly by the Soviet Union, in recent times mainly by the United States.

A third factor inhibiting decisive action is that those who framed the Charter anticipated that most wars in the post-war world would be international conflicts of the kind encountered between the wars. The fact that Article 2(7) of the Charter denied the United Nations the right to "intervene in matters that are essentially within the domestic jurisdiction of a member state" was thus not expected to inhibit significantly the organisation's capacity to maintain the peace. But in practice, as we have seen, a very large proportion of all the wars that have occurred since 1945 have taken place entirely or almost entirely within the frontiers of a single state. While the United Nations has been willing to take action over a considerable number of these cases, especially where there was some evidence of external involvement (for example, over the civil wars in Greece, Lebanon in 1958, the Congo and Yemen), it has ignored many others even if the evidence of external involvement was considerable.

A final reason why the United Nations has failed even to consider a substantial number of conflict situations in recent times, let alone to resolve them effectively, is that in a number of cases alternative channels have been used. Sometimes regional organisations or local groups are believed to be more appropriate: such as the OAS in the case of some Latin American disputes, the OAU in relation to Africa, or ASEAN in relation to South-East Asia. In other cases bilateral procedures for settlement may be under way which it is believed might be prejudiced by UN debate: as in the case of US efforts to secure settlements in Southern Africa, in Lebanon and in the Middle East generally, or French intervention in relation to Chad. Though the use of bilateral and regional procedures where appropriate was always envisaged in the Charter, the balance between the two has been significantly altered, and the role of the United Nations therefore substantially downgraded. Especially where a conflict occurs in the near vicinity of a superpower, or indeed any major power, that state may prefer to seek to find a solution on its own account and discourage discussion within international bodies.

These are only a few of the more obvious reasons why the collective security arrangements set out in the Charter have not been used by the United Nations, especially over recent years. But, even without being able to take action under Chapter VII, the organisation might have been able to take action of other kinds. That opportunity also has been lost.

The failure to use the Charter

Because no Security Council force has been established, the procedures set out in Chapter VII — that is, the use of sanctions, including the use of force, against an aggressor — have never been used to maintain the peace.* As a result of the failure of the negotiations which took place in 1946–7, the organisation gave up the idea, widespread at its foundation and implicit in its Charter, that it would be able to keep the peace by taking collective action against an aggressor (though there was no obvious reason why such action should not have been taken by the combined national forces of member states). That idea, the central tenet of the collective security ideal, has been in effect abandoned by the membership, just as it was abandoned, to the derision of many observers, by the majority in the League of Nations 40 years earlier. Just as members of the League found countless reasons for not taking military action against Japan when it invaded Manchuria in 1931, or against Italy when it invaded Ethiopia in 1935 — that is, for not taking up arms "to preserve as against external aggression the territorial integrity and existing political independence" of a state under attack — so members of the United Nations found equally cogent reasons for not joining in collective action against those states which committed acts of aggression, in far greater numbers, in the post-war world. Even in the case of Korea, where a specific recommendation was made by the Security Council, less than a third of the membership joined in defending the state under attack. In the other 120-odd wars of the period the Council has not even attempted to bring about such a response: not even attempted, in other words, to put into practice the collective security principle established in the Charter. In the mid 1980s about 20 wars were taking place in different parts of the world — in Nicaragua, El Salvador,

* Sanctions were introduced against Rhodesia in 1967, but these were seen not as a means of maintaining the peace, but as a means of persuading the Smith government to return to constitutional rule and to negotiate for a transfer of power.

Surinam, Western Sahara, Ethiopia (two wars), Somalia, Uganda, Angola, Mozambique, Lebanon, the Gulf, Sri Lanka, Afghanistan, Cambodia, Burma (three wars), East Timor and West Papua — without any attempt by the membership to apply any of the sanctions so carefully provided in the Charter. Where such wars have occurred member states have contented themselves with sporadic meetings to consider them; with the passage of grandiloquent resolutions addressed to the participants; at best, with proposing the appointment of a mediator or inviting the Secretary-General to take what steps he thought fit. But they have remained consistently unwilling to face the unpleasant and arduous responsibility of themselves intervening to maintain the peace.

In the light of this reluctance to put into practice Chapter VII of the Charter, it might be thought that member states would have tried instead to activate the alternative mechanism laid down for dealing with threats to the peace: that established in Chapter VI. This empowers the Security Council to "investigate any dispute or any situation which might lead to international friction or give rise to a dispute" (Article 34), to determine whether it is likely to endanger international peace and security and, if so, to propose appropriate action; to recomend "appropriate procedures or methods of adjustment" for a conflict (Article 36(1)); to refer a dispute to the International Court of Justice (Article 36(3)); if the dispute is likely to endanger international peace and security, "to recommend such terms of settlement as it may consider appropriate" (Article 37); or to "make recommendations to the parties with a view to a pacific settlement of the dispute (Article 38). The obvious advantage of these procedures is that they are designed to tackle disputes *before* they reach the stage of armed conflict; and so, if recourse had been had to them, they might, as intended, have prevented disputes from ever reaching that stage.

Extraordinarily, however, after a few half-hearted attempts in its early years, the Security Council has made no more use of the procedures contained in Chapter VI than it has of those in Chapter VII. To have taken such steps would have placed no onerous obligations on member states. They would not have been obliged to undertake lavish expenditure, to reach agonising political decisions, still less risk the lives of their own armed forces. They were required only to decide that it might be advisable to open an inquiry, appoint a sub-commission, initiate a mediation process, recommend a particular course of action or a particular type of settlement to the member states in question. For whatever reason — lassitude, caution, improvidence, lack of imagination — member states have, for the most part, been unwilling to contemplate even these innocuous and uncontentious steps. In most cases they have made no attempt to consider disputes and situations of tension before they have reached the stage of open war. And when they have done so — after it was already too late for effective action — they have contented themselves with imploring demands for a cease-fire, a withdrawal of forces or a miraculous reconciliation, such as nations at war are rarely disposed to contemplate.

This inactivity represents an extraordinary abandonment of the responsibilities which were placed on the Security Council in the Charter. The response made by the Council to threats to the peace has been spasmodic and uncertain. Most such threats are rarely considered until it is too late for constructive action to be taken. In effect the Council has downgraded itself to being a passive observer of the international scene, rather than an active participant. The assumption usually seems to be that, if any effective action is to be taken — to calm a crisis, to resolve a quarrel, or to set in motion a mediation — it will probably have to be undertaken outside the framework of the organisation: for example by a "trouble-shooter" sent by a super-power or through the action of some regional organisation, while the organisation set up precisely for those purposes remains inactive and impotent. In effect that organisation has decided to commit a kind of voluntary euthanasia.

If by some miracle a majority of members of the Security Council were to decide that they wished after all to exercise some of the functions the Charter has laid down for the Council, in other words to bring it to life again, what are the steps which they would need to take to bring that resurrection about?

The peaceful settlement of disputes

Member states, if they had that aim, might begin by re-examining the various provisions concerning the "pacific settlement of disputes" that the Charter itself proposes.

The first need would be to remind themselves that the responsibility for calling on the Council to consider a particular dispute is not confined to those states which are themselves involved in it, but that, under Article 35, "any member of the United Nations may bring any dispute, or any situation [which might lead to international friction of give rise to dispute] to the attention of the Security Council or of the General Assembly". This provision was included in the Charter precisely to ensure that all conflict situations were considered by the organisation, and considered at an early stage. It was on those grounds deliberately laid down that a call to the Council should not depend on the decisions of the two or more states most directly involved. The system was, in other words, based on the conception of a common interest among all the members in world order. On that basis it was accepted that it was in many cases for third parties — the bystanders — whether acting singly or collectively, to bring any threatening situation to the attention of the international community: that is, to the UN bodies responsible. This would eliminate the danger that, if the parties most directly involved felt, for whatever reasons of their own, under no compulsion to bring about a public discussion of their dispute (as in the case of the United States, the Soviet Union and North and South Vietnam — both non-members of the organisation — in the mid 1960s, and Iraq and Iran in 1980), other states, which had no good reason for wishing to evade the issue, would ensure that this none the less took place. Only if that were done, and the organisation was thus involved at an early stage, was it likely to be possible to institute the series of procedures for peaceful settlement so carefully provided for in Chapter VI of the Charter. The failure of members to take their responsibilities seriously meant that the kind of third-party influence provided for in the Charter has not been brought to bear at the only time when it could be expected to have some effect: before war broke out.

If the organisation were to be called in in this way at an early stage, members would be in a position to consider setting in motion one of the series of procedures listed in Article 33 of the Charter: "negotiation, enquiry, mediation, conciliation, arbitration, judicial settlement or resort to regional agencies or arrangements". This is a reasonably wide range of alternatives, and it would be surprising if there were not one of them which was appropriate for the particular conflict in question. The Security Council might in those circumstances, as that Article suggests, "call upon the parties to settle their dispute" by one of these means. In its early years the Council did sometimes make recommendations for negotiations among the parties (as following India's complaint about the treatment of people of Indian origin in South Africa); or for mediation (as over Kashmir); or for judicial settlement (the Corfu Channel case) or resort to a regional organisation (Guatemala's appeal in 1954, Cuba's appeals in 1960–1, the Dominican Republic in 1965). Today, for some reason that is unexplained, the Council virtually never makes any such proposal.

But there are other, and more positive, steps which the Council might take, under the provisions of Chapter VI of the Charter, to resolve disputes. It could for example follow the proposal of Article 34 that it should itself "investigate disputes or situations which might lead to friction or give rise to a dispute". One might expect that an organisation charged with maintaining the peace would quite frequently feel the need to call in this way for reports setting out, in relatively objective fashion, the basic facts of an issue and its background. In fact, although the Secretariat is asked to provide a vast range of reports in the economic and social field, it is virtually never called on to provide reports about the facts surrounding a threat to the peace. This is of course partly because the Council normally discusses such disputes only when they have already ceased to be a "threat" to the peace, when such a report might be valuable, and have become a "breach" of the peace or "act of aggression", when the usefulness of a report is much less. Even without a Secretariat report, however, the Council could itself, both before and after a war has broken out, institute an investigation of the kind called for in Article 34: for example, by setting up a small sub-commission of three or four member states to look at a particular dispute to uncover the basic facts. One of the main advantages of this procedure is that it would at least secure from the principal parties a clear account of their own approach to the quarrel, and their principal grounds for grievance against their antagonists. This in turn might enable the sub-commission to undertake a useful mediating function. Once more this is a procedure that was used by the organisation occasionally in its first decade or so — for example, over Indonesia in 1947, Palestine in the same year, and Kashmir in 1948. It is a procedure which has now fallen out of use. It could be revived with considerable advantage.

Other provisions of the Charter have been equally disregarded. Under Article 36 the Council may recommend to the parties "appropriate procedures or methods of adjustment". A direct proposal that two countries in dispute should adopt a particular procedure for settlement might sometimes be difficult for them to ignore when delivered with the full weight of the Council (for instance, in the disputes between Iraq and Iran in 1980, Argentina and Britain in 1982, Turkey and Greece in 1986). Here too, therefore, it is surprising that the Charter's provisions are not more often adopted by the Council. In extreme cases, when a dispute is thought likely to endanger international peace and security, the Council may (under Article 37) go beyond this and recommend "such terms of settlement as it may consider appropriate". This is in effect what the Council did in adopting the famous Resolution 242 on the Middle East in 1967: a resolution which has remained for 20 years as an indication of the kind of reasonable compromise settlement the international community regards as just, and the yardstick by which all national positions of the parties are judged. This too, therefore, may be a procedure which could more often be employed where it is desirable to demonstrate to the countries in dispute what reasonable outsiders see as a fair settlement.

But there is another Charter provision which, if the Council is to be brought into action at an earlier stage, needs to be more consistently implemented. Under Article 99 the Secretary-General may "bring to the attention of the Security-

Council any matter which in his opinion may threaten the maintenance of international peace and security". Here too the Charter terms are almost never put into effect. Successive Secretary-Generals have been most reluctant to use their powers under Article 99. They have been content to await action by member states to bring conflict situations before the Council; and this, as we have seen, means in practice to wait usually until after war has already broken out. Yet the Secretary-General was seen by founders of the organisation, above all by Roosevelt, as having a key role as the "world's moderator", a watchdog on behalf of humanity, who would ensure that the inter-governmental bodies of the organisation undertook the task laid down for them in the Charter. Of the organisation's five Secretary-Generals, Hammarskjöld has come nearest to fulfilling this role; but even he was extremely cautious in using his powers under Article 99. The furthest that most of his successors have been willing to go in demonstrating any independence of action is in appointing "special representatives", to seek solutions by unpublicised negotiations with the parties to a conflict (as over Cyprus, Afghanistan and the Gulf War in recent years). But (as each of these three cases demonstrates) this too occurs usually only after war has broken out; and even then is normally undertaken in leisurely fashion, over a period of years, without any spectacular progress becoming visible. Far more likely to be productive would be invitations to the parties to hold discussions, under the auspices of the Secretary-General himself, in UN headquarters in New York. Once again, it is surprising that procedures which have proved so successful in the past have been so rarely made use of in more recent times.

If the Secretary-General is to play a more active role of this kind, he may require better facilities than he has at his disposal at present. He now has to rely on the expertise and knowledge of a handful of officials based at UN headquarters in New York. His ability to acquire accurate knowledge of the situation on the ground in crisis areas would be increased if he could rely on facilities comparable to those at the disposal of the foreign minister of a national state. For this purpose he might require UN "ambassadors" at least in key capitals or regions of the world, able to send regular and detailed appreciations of crisis situations; together with sufficient staff in New York to process these reports and draft evaluations for the Secretary-General and the Security Council. The representative of the Secretary-General abroad should be in a position to make representations direct to the foreign ministers of the states of the region, and, conversely, to transmit their views direct to him in New York. The information provided in this way, for the use of the Security Council as much as the Secretary-General, would enable them to play a far more active and pre-emptive role, at a much earlier stage, than they are generally content to play today.

A further change that is necessary if the Security Council is to play a more effective part than it now does is for more of the work of the Council to be undertaken in private. The public meetings of the Council are of course only the visible tip of an iceberg, much of which is buried under a sea of secret diplomacy. In many cases the open sessions are preceded by a considerable amount of confidential discussions in the corridors or in the rooms of the current President. But, so long as all are aware that they are preparing for a public confrontation, under the glare of the television lights, much of the value of this consultation is destroyed. It may appear more important to score valuable debating points against opponents, in a highly publicised forum, than to explore the possibilities for the settlement of a long-standing international dispute. So long as it remains a public spectacle, the Council is inevitably seen by the world as a whole as an arena of conflict rather than a chamber for conciliation; a cockpit, in which fierce and highly publicised battles are fought out, rather than a court in which private settlements are arrived at. In consequence it not only loses authority and respect. It forfeits the opportunity to explore compromise solutions and secure lasting settlements.

If the role of the organisation in meeting breaches of the peace is to be enhanced, it may also be necessary to expand its capacity for peace-keeping. Peace-keeping operations have until today been undertaken entirely on an *ad hoc* basis. No provisions were made for them in the UN Charter (which provided only for "enforcement action" — that is, operations where UN forces were expected to have to fight to defeat an aggressor). In practice, when the need for a peace-keeping force has arisen, it has always proved possible to put one together; and this is likely to remain the case in future. But the better prepared the member states are in advance for such operations, the more willingly they will respond in future situations where they may be required. Arrangements by member states to train contingents specially for peace-keeping operations, or for joint training and manoeuvres among several such countries, are therefore valuable. The ancient argument, undertaken mainly in the so-called Committee of 33, about the authorisation and control of peace-keeping forces is unlikely to be resolved. But this is of little consequence, since the precedents already built up, in seven such operations over the past 30 years, provide adequate guidelines for the future. The most contentious, and potentially damaging, dispute has concerned financing. And it is important that the compromise reached in 1974, under which all members shared in contributing to the Sinai force, outside the regular budget but on an agreed scale, should be maintained to provide a secure financial basis for future operations.

If the authority of the United Nations is to be restored, unspectacular yet significant procedural changes of this kind may have an important role to play.

Authority without power

It is not only modern super-powers, therefore, which find it extremely difficult in contemporary conditions to secure their ends by the deployment of superior armed power. The United Nations too, though for different reasons, is equally unable to impose its authority, as was hoped at its foundation, by the threat, or even use, of military force. It too must depend, like them, on *political* rather than military means: on influence rather than coercion. To secure its ends, therefore, it needs to find the means of maximising the influence it can exercise in default of power.

It has manifestly not succeeded in that task at present. It has failed to make itself a predictable and visible presence in world affairs which is able to influence the actions of states and which must be carefully taken account of by all governments in their conduct of their foreign relations. It was intended to be an organisation that would have a general and continuing responsibility for maintaining world peace and resolving conflicts among states as they arose. It has become an organisation which undertakes that function only fitfully, and only when called on to do so by particular member states. It is for this reason that the 20 or so wars taking place in different parts of the world today are uninfluenced, and for the most part not even considered, by the Security Council. Most have not been discussed at all; and the rest only briefly and without significant impact on their course. Still less were the situations which led to those wars confronted by the organisation, as the Charter lays down, before they erupted into armed conflict. The United Nations today, therefore, makes no attempt to act, as was assumed in its early years, as a watchdog, continually monitoring the situation and taking whatever steps are necessary to reduce tensions and prevent war. Instead it has become a body which meets spasmodically, when an aggrieved state chooses to stir it to life, and which acts, even then, as a forum for public wrangling rather than private deliberation; for competitive point-scoring rather than objective judgement or calm conciliation. In the eyes of the public, it is not an impartial authority, expressing the views of disinterested outsiders on the best means of resolving particular conflicts, but a highly political body, enunciating the viewpoint of the current majority on the Council, in sometimes partisan and always highly publicised resolutions, which have little impact on those most directly concerned and rapidly lose whatever relevance they once had.

It is scarcely surprising, therefore, that respect for the United Nations has progressively declined. But for an authority which seeks to exercise authority without power, to win compliance without coercion, respect is the essential requirement. To secure that respect, among governments and peoples alike, the organisation needs to operate in a very different way. It needs to undertake a far more continuous oversight of world affairs than it does at present; to establish its presence far more visibly in the discussion of world affairs; and to adopt a far more impartial and objective position. Above all, it needs to show that it is concerned not simply with short-term opinions and ephemeral resolutions, but with the more long-term task of seeking, through sustained behind-the-scenes negotiations, in which the parties most directly concerned would have a part, the means of resolving particular conflict situations. In other words, it needs to show that its concern is conciliation rather than confrontation.

This would represent a significant change in the ways that the organisation perates. That change could come about only if the policies of its *members* were altered. A call for a change in the United Nations is not a demand for a change in some remote entity, existing somewhere up in the clouds, but a demand for a change in the actions of states. What the organisation does and what it is are what the member states decide it should do and be. It remains the case, as a former British representative at the United Nations used to declare, that "there is nothing wrong with the United Nations except its members". Every fault that can be laid at the door of the organisation is one that its members have wished on it. And, if those members desire a more peaceful international society, and a more effective world organisation to maintain peace within it, it is they, and they alone, who are in a position to bring it about.

Conclusions: The Limits of Military Power

What we have observed in these pages is a paradox. The major states of the modern world dispose of a power unmatched in former times. They control weapons of supreme sophistication, vast complexity and unimaginable destructiveness. They can deploy a fire-power a million times greater than that which any state could boast only 50 years ago. They can pulverise villages, towns and entire cities, and kill millions of their enemies' populations, in an instant. Yet this capability is of no value. It does not enable them to achieve any of their aims. Their weapons are too powerful to be useful. They can destroy and kill and maim. But they do not make it possible for those countries to impose their will on other states.

This is not, as is popularly believed, because they themselves are vulnerable to the same weapons in reverse. The states of every age have been vulnerable in that sense. In seeking victory they have always risked defeat, and all the penalties that go with it. Although defeat today involves a destruction infinitely greater than in former times (whether or not nuclear weapons are employed), it might still be risked if victory were believed more probable. In any case, the imbalance of power is in many cases such that major states have no need to fear retaliation of that kind. Yet even in that situation their more powerful weapons remain unused. It is not fear, in other words, that restrains them from making use of the armed force that is available to them.

The real change is that no victory is to be won even to the side that prevails in such a contest. The destruction of another state would not bring the prizes which are valued by leaders in the modern world. The ultimate aims of modern leaders are political. They do not seek territory or colonies or preferential trading rights, like their predecessors only a century ago. They want to see a victory for the political system in which they believe. They want to see particular governments overthrown, or new ones brought to power, in other states. But military victory (even if it can be won) cannot easily secure these goals. Those outcomes can be achieved only if the population in the territory concerned, or at least the more influential sections of it, can be persuaded to share their views concerning the way they should be governed.

Such persuasion is not easy. The lesson of Vietnam and Afghanistan is only too clear to see. Even the most powerful states on earth, armed with all the vast array of modern weaponry, cannot easily convince by acts of force. However many bombs they rain down, they will not quickly persuade the people on the receiving end — even a people far less well armed and infinitely weaker — to accept their own political objecives. The battle for hearts and minds is not so easily won. If it is to be won at all, it is not with bombs and tanks and helicopter gunships, however numerous they are and however modern their design.

The task of persuasion is more arduous and more time-consuming. It is not to be achieved by the quick fix: the lightning *coup d'état* or the rapid conquest. Political objectives can be achieved only by political means. And, in a world where the principal aims of states are political, it is not, therefore, bigger armies and more powerful and sophisticated weapons which secure success, but more effective influence. It is better powers of persuasion, not military power, which states most require to secure their ends in the modern international political system.

The power to persuade successfully requires above all a coherent political philosophy which will carry conviction among the masses of people whose voice will be ultimately decisive. The claim to speak for "democracy" is already something: if you wish for the support of the mass of people, it is clearly useful to claim a voice for the mass of the people in the way they are governed. But it is not enough. Democracy means many different things to different people; and there is today no political group on earth, from Stalinist Communists to Islamic fundamentalists, who do not claim to stand for a more "democratic" system and a better voice for the mass of the people. What matters, therefore, is not the championing of democracy, but what kind of democracy is championed. To proclaim the virtues of "democracy" will not necessarily produce ardent adherents if it means a call for the type of elections which legitimised the power of a Marcos, a Somoza or a Pinochet, or of a judicial system which cheerfully enforces their laws, or of a "free press" which is owned and controlled by supporters of such rulers. To uphold the benefits of a parliamentary system while refusing demands for a fairer distribution of land and other basic necessities will not win instant support in places — such as Central America, South-East Asia and parts of Africa — where what ordinary people need and demand is not votes but the right to produce their food for their own family rather than for the landlord or the multinational company, a living wage, or simply enough to eat. The West will not win a battle for hearts and minds, therefore, unless it produces a definition of democracy more relevant to the needs of ordinary people, in the 120 countries where such struggles take place, than those produced by some of its best-known ideologues today.

If this is the nature of the battle which takes place among states today, there are other implications for the contemporary international political system. If persuasion rather than coercion is the ultimate objective, it becomes important to ensure that there are appropriate channels through which persuasion can be undertaken. At present the institutions which exist for resolving conflict and exchanging influence are manifestly deficient. Super-power diplomacy is spasmodic and irregular, constantly at the mercy of the current political winds, and insufficiently representative of important voices within the world community. Such contacts need to be institutionalised in a way that they are not today. "Summits", for example, should take place at regular intervals rather than according to the mood of the moment. They need to be broadened to include important centres of power and population — Western Europe, China, Japan and the third world — which are at present excluded. The United Nations, which at present ignores, or makes a totally inadequate response to, many of the world's chief conflict situations — and even fails to make use of the procedures laid down in its own Charter — needs to be radically overhauled if it is to be able to undertake the tasks which its founders laid down for it.

It is too easy to say that all that is needed to reduce conflict in the modern world is to reduce intervention. The world is too small for the people of one state to be indifferent to what happens in the next. The real question concerns the *kind* of intervention. The simplest way to reduce international conflict and the wars of the modern world would be by a strengthening of sovereignty, sufficient to prevent the type of interventions which are the principal cause of armed conflict in the modern world. But such a strengthening of sovereignty would increase the vulnerability of subject populations to all-powerful governments abusing their power by the imprisonment, torture and killing of thousands of innocent people. To sanction the use of force for the defence of human rights would open the way to still more wars of intervention, often undertaken, whatever the justifications given, for blatantly self-interested reasons. This is another area where the fundamental problem is political rather than military; where it is persuasion rather than coercion which is ultimately required. Here again it is international action — a strengthening of international institutions to enable the pressures of world opinion to be mobilised more effectively — rather than unilateral action which is needed if the protection of human rights is to be undertaken more effectively than it is today.

The use of force is always most attractive today, as in earlier times, to those who believe they know best what is right for others and for the world as a whole. Force is necessary, it is nearly always alleged, not to promote a national interest but to fulfil a moral duty: not for the people of the United States but for the people of Vietnam, not for the people of the United Arab Republic but for the people of Yemen, not for the people of the Soviet Union but for the people of Afghanistan. The experience of the modern world, however, is that, even for those laudable purposes, it is ineffective. Such ventures — whether or not those were genuinely the aims which motivated them (which is not self-evident) — have almost invariably failed.

Those who have political objectives to pursue — in other words, most of the governments of the modern world — today require different methods to achieve their purposes: methods that are more complex, more difficult, more challenging, but ultimately more effective, than the crude, mindless bludgeonings of armed power alone.

BOOK LIST

Chapter 1   The Erosion of Military Power

Brodie, Bernard, *War and Politics* (New York, 1973).
Buchan, Alastair, *War in Modern Society* (London, 1966).
Claude, Inis, *Power in International Relations* (New York, 1962).
Dunn, K. A., and Standenmaier, W. A., *Alternative Military Strategies for the Future* (Boulder, Col., 1985).
Hoffman, Stanley, *The State of War* (London, 1965).
Howard, Michael (ed.), *The Theory and Practice of War* (London, 1965).
Luard, Evan, *War in International Society* (London, 1986).
Quester, G. H. (ed.), *Power, Action and Interaction* (Boston, Mass., 1971).
Schelling, Thomas, *Arms and Influence* (New Haven, Conn., 1966).
Stoessinger, J. G., *The Might of Nations: Politics in our Time*, 6th edn (New York, 1979).
Thompson, Robert, *Revolutionary War in World Strategy* (London, 1973).
Wood, D., *Conflict in the Twentieth Century* (London, 1968).

Chapter 2   The Irrelevance of Nuclear Weapons

Alford, J. (ed.), *Arms Control and European Security* (London, 1984).
Bechhoefer, B. C., *Post-war Negotiations on Arms Control* (London, 1982).
Bertram, C., *Mutual Force Reductions in Europe* (London, 1972).
Burt, R. (ed.), *Arms Control and Defense Postures in the 1980s* (Boulder, Col., 1982).
Carter, A. B., and Schwarz, D. N., *Ballistic Missile Defense* (Washington, DC, 1984).
Coffey, J. I., *Arms Control and European Security: A Guide to East–West Negotiations* (London, 1977).
European Security Study, *Strengthening Conventional Deterrence in Europe: Proposals for the 1980s* (New York, 1985).
Goldblat, Jozef, *Agreements on Arms Control* (London, 1982).

Howe, J. O'C. (ed.), *Armed Peace: The Search for World Security* (London, 1984).

Hyland, W. G., *et al.*, *Nuclear Weapons in Europe* (New York, 1984).

Nerlich, Uwe, *Nuclear Weapons and East–West Negotiations* (Oxford, 1983).

Ruehl, L., *M.B.F.R.: Lessons and Problems* (London, 1982).

Sheehan, M., *The Arms Race* (Oxford, 1983).

Tinman, John (ed.), *The Fallacy of Star Wars* (New York, 1984).

Treverton, G., *Nuclear Weapons in Europe* (London, 1981).

United Nations, *The United Nations and Disarmament 1945–70* (New York, 1970).

——, *Study on Conventional Disarmament* (New York, 1985).

Winkler, T. D., *Arms Control and the Politics of European Security* (London, 1982).

Chapter 3   The Localisation of Warfare

Ayoob, M. (ed.), *Conflict and Intervention in the Third World* (New York, 1980).

Blomfield, L. B., and Leiss, A. C., *Controlling Small Wars* (London, 1969).

Deitchman, S. J., *Limited War and American Defense* (Cambridge, Mass., 1969).

Griffiths, W. E., *The Superpowers and Regional Tensions* (Lexington, Mass., 1982).

Halperin, Morton, *Limited War in the Nuclear Age* (New York, 1963).

Kitson, Frank, *Low Intensity Operations: Subversion, Insurgency and Peacekeeping* (London, 1971).

Luard, Evan, *Conflict and Peace in the Modern International System*, 2nd edn (London, 1988).

McClintock, R., *The Meaning of Limited War* (Boston, Mass., 1967).

O'Neill, Robert, and Horner, D. M. (eds), *New Directions in Strategic Thinking* (London, 1981).

O'Neill, Robert, and Ball, D. (eds), *Strategy and Defence* (London, 1982).

Summers, H. G., *On Strategy: A Critical Analysis of the Vietnam War* (Novato, Calif., 1982).

Taylor, Maxwell D., *The Uncertain Trumpet* (New York, 1959).

Taylor, William J., and Mearnen, S. A., *The Future of Conflict in the 1980s* (Lexington, Mass., 1983).

Chapter 4 The Failure of Interventionism

Barnet, R., *Intervention and Revolution: The United States in the Third World* (New York, 1968).

Blasier, C., *The Hovering Giant: U.S. Responses to Revolutionary Change in Latin America* (Pittsburgh, 1976).

Blechman, B., and Kaplan, S. (eds), *Forces without War: U.S. Armed Forces as a Political Instrument* (Washington, DC, 1978).

Bull, Hedley (ed.), *Intervention in World Politics* (Oxford, 1984).

Hosmer, S., and Wolfe, T., *Soviet Policy and Practice towards Third World Conflicts* (Lexington, Mass., 1982).

Katz, M., *The Third World in Soviet Military Thought* (London, 1982).

Little, R., *External Intervention in Civil Wars* (London, 1975).

Luard, Evan (ed.), *The International Regulation of Civil Wars* (London, 1970).

McFarlane, Neil, *Super-power Rivalry and Third World Radicalism* (London, 1985).

——, *Intervention and Regional Security* (London, 1985).

Rosenau, D. M. (ed.), *The International Aspects of Civil Strife* (Princeton, NJ, 1964).

Chapter 5 The Super-power Relationship

Bell, Coral, *The Diplomacy of Detente* (London, 1977).

Brown, Colin, and Mooney, P. J., *Cold War to Detente* (London, 1976).

Garthoff, Raymond L., *Detente and Confrontation: American–Soviet Relations from Nixon to Reagan* (Washington, DC, 1985).

Hoffman, Stanley, *Primacy or World Order* (New York, 1978).

Holbrand, C. (ed.), *Superpowers and International Conflict* (London, 1979).

Hyland, G., and Sonnerfeldt, H., *Soviet Perspectives on Security* (New York, 1979).

Kaufman, E., *The Superpowers and their Spheres of Influence* (London, 1976).

O'Neill, Robert (ed.), *The Conduct of East–West Relations in the 1980s* (London, 1985).

Sloss, L., and Scott-Davis, M., *A Game for High Stakes: Lessons Learned in Negotiating with the Soviet Union* (Cambridge, Mass., 1986).

Chapter 6 The Role of Western Europe

Burgess, W. R., and Huntley, J. R., *Europe and America in the Next Ten Years* (New York, 1970).
Dyson, K., *European Detente* (London, 1986).
Freedman, L. (ed.), *The Troubled Alliance: Atlantic Relations in the 1980s* (London, 1983).
Holborn, H., *The Political Collapse of Europe* (New York, 1964).
Kissinger, H., *The Troubled Partnership: A Re-appraisal of the Atlantic Alliance* (London, 1965).
Mendl, W., *Western Europe and Japan between the Superpowers* (London, 1984).
Nairn, T. (ed.), *Atlantic Europe: The Radical View* (Amsterdam, 1976).
Porte, A. de, *Europe between the Super Powers* (New York, 1976).
Taylor, Trevor, *European Defence Cooperation* (London, 1984).
Treverton, G. F., *Making the Alliance Work: The United States and Western Europe* (London, 1985).
Wallace, William, *Foreign Policymaking in Western Europe* (Farnborough, Hants, 1978).
Wallace, William and Helen, *Policymaking in the European Community*, 2nd edn (London, 1983).

Chapter 7 The Changing United Nations

Bailey, Sydney, *The United Nations: A Short Political Guide* (London, 1963).
——, *The General Assembly of the United Nations* (London, 1960).
——, *The Procedure of the UN Security Council* (Oxford, 1975).
——, *The Secretariat of the United Nations* (London, 1964).
Coyle, D. C., *The United Nations and How it Works* (New York, 1969).
Padelford, N. J., and Goodrich, L. M., *The United Nations in the Balance* (New York, 1965).
Kay, David A., *The United Nations Political System* (New York, 1967).
Luard, Evan, *The United Nations: How it Works and What it Does* (London, 1978).

Chapter 8 Keeping the Peace

Berridge, G. R., and Jennings, A., *Diplomacy at the UN* (London, 1985).

Goodrich, L. M., and Simons, A. P., *The United Nations and the Maintenance of International Peace and Security* (Westpoint, Conn., 1955).

Gordenker, Leon, *The UN Secretary-General and the Maintenance of Peace* (New York, 1967).

Hammarskjöld, Dag, *The Servant of Peace: A Selection of Speeches and Statements* (New York, 1962).

Higgins, Rosalyn, *United Nations Peacekeeping 1946–67* (London, 1969–81).

James, Alan, *The Politics of Peacekeeping* (London, 1969).

Murphy, J. F., *The United Nations and the Control of International Violence* (Manchester, 1983).

Nicholson, David, *The UN Secretary-General: Towards Greater Effectiveness* (New York, 1982).

Wainhouse, David, *International Peacekeeping at the Crossroads* (Washington, DC, 1973).

Wiseman, H., *Peacekeeping: Appraisals and Prospects* (London, 1983).

Index